TESS OF THE D'URBERVILLES

Thomas Hardy

SPARKNOTES is a registered trademark of SparkNotes LLC.

Spark Publishing
A Division of Barnes & Noble
120 Fifth Avenue
New York, NY 10011
www.sparknotes.com

ISBN-13: 978-1-5866-3382-0
ISBN-10: 1-5866-3382-1

Please submit changes or report errors to www.sparknotes.com/errors.

Printed and bound in the United States

7 9 10 8

Introduction:
Stopping to Buy SparkNotes on a Snowy Evening

Whose words these are you *think* you know.
Your paper's due tomorrow, though;
We're glad to see you stopping here
To get some help before you go.

Lost your course? You'll find it here.
Face tests and essays without fear.
Between the words, good grades at stake:
Get great results throughout the year.

Once school bells caused your heart to quake
As teachers circled each mistake.
Use SparkNotes and no longer weep,
Ace every single test you take.

Yes, books are lovely, dark, and deep,
But only what you grasp you keep,
With hours to go before you sleep,
With hours to go before you sleep.

CONTENTS

CONTEXT   1

PLOT OVERVIEW   3

CHARACTER LIST   5

ANALYSIS OF MAJOR CHARACTERS   9
    TESS DURBEYFIELD   9
    ALEC D'URBERVILLE   10
    ANGEL CLARE   11

THEMES, MOTIFS & SYMBOLS   13
    THE INJUSTICE OF EXISTENCE   13
    CHANGING IDEAS OF SOCIAL CLASS
        IN VICTORIAN ENGLAND   14
    MEN DOMINATING WOMEN   14
    BIRDS   15
    THE BOOK OF GENESIS   16
    VARIANT NAMES   16
    PRINCE   17
    THE D'URBERVILLE FAMILY VAULT   18
    BRAZIL   18

SUMMARY & ANALYSIS   19
    PHASE THE FIRST: THE MAIDEN
        CHAPTERS I–III   19
        CHAPTERS IV–VII   21
        CHAPTERS VIII–XI   24
    PHASE THE SECOND: MAIDEN NO MORE
        CHAPTERS XII–XV   27
    PHASE THE THIRD: THE RALLY
        CHAPTERS XVI–XIX   29
        CHAPTERS XX–XXIV   32
    PHASE THE FOURTH: THE CONSEQUENCE
        CHAPTERS XXV–XXXI   34
        CHAPTERS XXXII–XXXIV   37

PHASE THE FIFTH: THE WOMAN PAYS
    CHAPTERS XXXV–XXXIX   40
    CHAPTERS XL–XLIV   42
PHASE THE SIXTH: THE CONVERT
    CHAPTERS XLV–XLVIII   45
    CHAPTERS XLIX–LII   48
PHASE THE SEVENTH: THE FULFILLMENT
    CHAPTERS LIII–LIX   51

IMPORTANT QUOTATIONS EXPLAINED   55

KEY FACTS   61

STUDY QUESTIONS & ESSAY TOPICS   63

REVIEW & RESOURCES   67
    QUIZ   67
    SUGGESTIONS FOR FURTHER READING   72

CONTEXT

THOMAS HARDY WAS BORN on June 2, 1840, in Higher Bockhampton in Dorset, a rural region of southwestern England that was to become the focus of his fiction. The child of a builder, Hardy was apprenticed at the age of sixteen to John Hicks, an architect who lived in the city of Dorchester. The location would later serve as the model for Hardy's fictional Casterbridge. Although he gave serious thought to attending university and entering the church, a struggle he would dramatize in his novel *Jude the Obscure,* declining religious faith and lack of money led Hardy to pursue a career in writing instead. He spent nearly a dozen years toiling in obscurity and producing unsuccessful novels and poetry. *Far from the Madding Crowd,* published in 1874, was the author's first critical and financial success. Finally able to support himself as a writer, Hardy married Emma Lavinia Gifford later that year.

Although he built a reputation as a successful novelist, Hardy considered himself first and foremost a poet. To him, novels were primarily a means of earning a living. Like many of his contemporaries, he first published his novels in periodic installments in magazines or serial journals, and his work reflects the conventions of serialization. To ensure that readers would buy a serialized novel, writers often structured each installment to be something of a cliffhanger, which explained the convoluted, often incredible plots of many such Victorian novels. But Hardy cannot solely be labeled a Victorian novelist. Nor can he be categorized simply as a Modernist, in the tradition of writers like Virginia Woolf or D. H. Lawrence, who were determined to explode the conventions of nineteenth-century literature and build a new kind of novel in its place. In many respects, Hardy was trapped in the middle ground between the nineteenth and twentieth centuries, between Victorian sensibilities and more modern ones, and between tradition and innovation.

Soon after *Tess of the d'Urbervilles* (1891) was published, its sales assured Hardy's financial future. But the novel also aroused a substantial amount of controversy. In *Tess of the d'Urbervilles* and other novels, Hardy demonstrates his deep sense of moral sympathy for England's lower classes, particularly for rural women. He became famous for his compassionate, often controversial portrayal of young women victimized by the self-righteous rigidity of English social morality. Perhaps his most famous depiction of such a young woman is in *Tess of the d'Urbervilles*. This novel and the one that followed it, *Jude the Obscure* (1895), engendered widespread public scandal with their comparatively frank look at the sexual hypocrisy of English society.

Hardy lived and wrote in a time of difficult social change, when England was making its slow and painful transition from an old-fashioned, agricultural nation to a modern, industrial one. Businessmen and entrepreneurs, or "new money," joined the ranks of the social elite, as some families of the ancient aristocracy, or "old money," faded into obscurity. Tess's family in *Tess of the d'Urbervilles* illustrates this change, as Tess's parents, the Durbeyfields, lose themselves in the fantasy of belonging to an ancient and aristocratic family, the d'Urbervilles. Hardy's novel strongly suggests that such a family history is not only meaningless but also utterly undesirable. Hardy's views on the subject were appalling to conservative and status-conscious British readers, and *Tess of the d'Urbervilles* was met in England with widespread controversy.

Hardy was frustrated by the controversy caused by his work, and he finally abandoned novel-writing altogether following *Jude the Obscure*. He spent the rest of his career writing poetry. Though today he is remembered somewhat more for his novels, he was an acclaimed poet in his time and was buried in the prestigious Poet's Corner of Westminster Abbey following his death in 1928.

Plot Overview

THE POOR PEDDLER JOHN DURBEYFIELD is stunned to learn that he is the descendent of an ancient noble family, the d'Urbervilles. Meanwhile, Tess, his eldest daughter, joins the other village girls in the May Day dance, where Tess briefly exchanges glances with a young man. Mr. Durbeyfield and his wife decide to send Tess to the d'Urberville mansion, where they hope Mrs. d'Urberville will make Tess's fortune. In reality, Mrs. d'Urberville is no relation to Tess at all: her husband, the merchant Simon Stokes, simply changed his name to d'Urberville after he retired. But Tess does not know this fact, and when the lascivious Alec d'Urberville, Mrs. d'Urberville's son, procures Tess a job tending fowls on the d'Urberville estate, Tess has no choice but to accept, since she blames herself for an accident involving the family's horse, its only means of income.

Tess spends several months at this job, resisting Alec's attempts to seduce her. Finally, Alec takes advantage of her in the woods one night after a fair. Tess knows she does not love Alec. She returns home to her family to give birth to Alec's child, whom she christens Sorrow. Sorrow dies soon after he is born, and Tess spends a miserable year at home before deciding to seek work elsewhere. She finally accepts a job as a milkmaid at the Talbothays Dairy.

At Talbothays, Tess enjoys a period of contentment and happiness. She befriends three of her fellow milkmaids—Izz, Retty, and Marian—and meets a man named Angel Clare, who turns out to be the man from the May Day dance at the beginning of the novel. Tess and Angel slowly fall in love. They grow closer throughout Tess's time at Talbothays, and she eventually accepts his proposal of marriage. Still, she is troubled by pangs of conscience and feels she should tell Angel about her past. She writes him a confessional note and slips it under his door, but it slides under the carpet and Angel never sees it.

After their wedding, Angel and Tess both confess indiscretions: Angel tells Tess about an affair he had with an older woman in London, and Tess tells Angel about her history with Alec. Tess forgives Angel, but Angel cannot forgive Tess. He gives her some money and boards a ship bound for Brazil, where he thinks he might establish a farm. He tells Tess he will try to accept her past but warns her not to try to join him until he comes for her.

Tess struggles. She has a difficult time finding work and is forced to take a job at an unpleasant and unprosperous farm. She tries to visit Angel's family but overhears his brothers discussing Angel's poor marriage, so she leaves. She hears a wandering preacher speak and is stunned to discover that he is Alec d'Urberville, who has been converted to Christianity by Angel's father, the Reverend Clare. Alec and Tess are each shaken by their encounter, and Alec appallingly begs Tess never to tempt him again. Soon after, however, he again begs Tess to marry him, having turned his back on his religious ways.

Tess learns from her sister Liza-Lu that her mother is near death, and Tess is forced to return home to take care of her. Her mother recovers, but her father unexpectedly dies soon after. When the family is evicted from their home, Alec offers help. But Tess refuses to accept, knowing he only wants to obligate her to him again.

At last, Angel decides to forgive his wife. He leaves Brazil, desperate to find her. Instead, he finds her mother, who tells him Tess has gone to a village called Sandbourne. There, he finds Tess in an expensive boardinghouse called The Herons, where he tells her he has forgiven her and begs her to take him back. Tess tells him he has come too late. She was unable to resist and went back to Alec d'Urberville. Angel leaves in a daze, and, heartbroken to the point of madness, Tess goes upstairs and stabs her lover to death. When the landlady finds Alec's body, she raises an alarm, but Tess has already fled to find Angel.

Angel agrees to help Tess, though he cannot quite believe that she has actually murdered Alec. They hide out in an empty mansion for a few days, then travel farther. When they come to Stonehenge, Tess goes to sleep, but when morning breaks shortly thereafter, a search party discovers them. Tess is arrested and sent to jail. Angel and Liza-Lu watch as a black flag is raised over the prison, signaling Tess's execution.

CHARACTER LIST

Tess Durbeyfield The novel's protagonist. Tess is a beautiful, loyal young woman living with her impoverished family in the village of Marlott. Tess has a keen sense of responsibility and is committed to doing the best she can for her family, although her inexperience and lack of wise parenting leave her extremely vulnerable. Her life is complicated when her father discovers a link to the noble line of the d'Urbervilles, and, as a result, Tess is sent to work at the d'Urberville mansion. Unfortunately, her ideals cannot prevent her from sliding further and further into misfortune after she becomes pregnant by Alec d'Urberville. The terrible irony is that Tess and her family are not really related to this branch of the d'Urbervilles at all: Alec's father, a merchant named Simon Stokes, simply assumed the name after he retired.

Angel Clare An intelligent young man who has decided to become a farmer to preserve his intellectual freedom from the pressures of city life. Angel's father and his two brothers are respected clergymen, but Angel's religious doubts have kept him from joining the ministry. He meets Tess when she is a milkmaid at the Talbothays Dairy and quickly falls in love with her.

Alec d'Urberville The handsome, amoral son of a wealthy merchant named Simon Stokes. Alec is not really a d'Urberville—his father simply took on the name of the ancient noble family after he built his mansion and retired. Alec is a manipulative, sinister young man who does everything he can to seduce the inexperienced Tess when she comes to work for his family. When he finally has his way with her, out in the woods, he subsequently tries to help her but is unable to make her love him.

Mr. John Durbeyfield Tess's father, a lazy peddler in Marlott. John is naturally quick, but he hates work. When he learns that he descends from the noble line of the d'Urbervilles, he is quick to make an attempt to profit from the connection.

Mrs. Joan Durbeyfield Tess's mother. Joan has a strong sense of propriety and very particular hopes for Tess's life. She is continually disappointed and hurt by the way in which her daughter's life actually proceeds. But she is also somewhat simpleminded and naturally forgiving, and she is unable to remain angry with Tess—particularly once Tess becomes her primary means of support.

Mrs. d'Urberville Alec's mother, and the widow of Simon Stokes. Mrs. d'Urberville is blind and often ill. She cares deeply for her animals, but not for her maid Elizabeth, her son Alec, nor Tess when she comes to work for her. In fact, she never sees Tess as anything more than an impoverished girl.

Marian, Izz Huett, and Retty Priddle Milkmaids whom Tess befriends at the Talbothays Dairy. Marian, Izz, and Retty remain close to Tess throughout the rest of her life. They are all in love with Angel and are devastated when he chooses Tess over them: Marian turns to drink, Retty attempts suicide, and Izz nearly runs off to Brazil with Angel when he leaves Tess. Nevertheless, they remain helpful to Tess. Marian helps her find a job at a farm called Flintcomb-Ash, and Marian and Izz write Angel a plaintive letter encouraging him to give Tess another chance.

Reverend Clare Angel's father, a somewhat intractable but principled clergyman in the town of Emminster. Mr. Clare considers it his duty to convert the populace. One of his most difficult cases proves to be none other than Alec d'Urberville.

Mrs. Clare Angel's mother, a loving but snobbish woman who places great stock in social class. Mrs. Clare wants Angel to marry a suitable woman, meaning a woman with the proper social, financial, and religious background. Mrs. Clare initially looks down on Tess as a "simple" and impoverished girl, but later grows to appreciate her.

Reverend Felix Clare Angel's brother, a village curate.

Reverend Cuthbert Clare Angel's brother, a classical scholar and dean at Cambridge. Cuthbert, who can concentrate only on university matters, marries Mercy Chant.

Eliza Louisa Durbeyfield Tess's younger sister. Tess believes Liza-Lu has all of Tess's own good qualities and none of her bad ones, and she encourages Angel to look after and even marry Liza-Lu after Tess dies.

Sorrow Tess's son with Alec d'Urberville. Sorrow dies in his early infancy, after Tess christens him herself. She later buries him herself as well, and decorates his grave.

Mercy Chant The daughter of a friend of the Reverend Clare. Mr. Clare hopes Angel will marry Mercy, but after Angel marries Tess, Mercy becomes engaged to his brother Cuthbert instead.

ANALYSIS OF MAJOR CHARACTERS

TESS DURBEYFIELD

Intelligent, strikingly attractive, and distinguished by her deep moral sensitivity and passionate intensity, Tess is indisputably the central character of the novel that bears her name. But she is also more than a distinctive individual: Hardy makes her into somewhat of a mythic heroine. Her name, formally Theresa, recalls St. Teresa of Avila, another martyr whose vision of a higher reality cost her her life. Other characters often refer to Tess in mythical terms, as when Angel calls her a "Daughter of Nature" in Chapter XVIII, or refers to her by the Greek mythological names "Artemis" and "Demeter" in Chapter XX. The narrator himself sometimes describes Tess as more than an individual woman, but as something closer to a mythical incarnation of womanhood. In Chapter XIV, he says that her eyes are "neither black nor blue nor grey nor violet; rather all these shades together," like "an almost standard woman." Tess's story may thus be a "standard" story, representing a deeper and larger experience than that of a single individual.

In part, Tess represents the changing role of the agricultural workers in England in the late nineteenth century. Possessing an education that her unschooled parents lack, since she has passed the Sixth Standard of the National Schools, Tess does not quite fit into the folk culture of her predecessors, but financial constraints keep her from rising to a higher station in life. She belongs in that higher world, however, as we discover on the first page of the novel with the news that the Durbeyfields are the surviving members of the noble and ancient family of the d'Urbervilles. There is aristocracy in Tess's blood, visible in her graceful beauty—yet she is forced to work as a farmhand and milkmaid. When she tries to express her joy by singing lower-class folk ballads at the beginning of the third part of the novel, they do not satisfy her—she seems not quite comfortable with those popular songs. But, on the other hand, her diction, while more polished than her mother's, is not quite up to the level of Alec's or Angel's. She is in between, both socially and culturally. Thus, Tess is a symbol of unclear and unstable notions of class in nineteenth-century Britain, where old family lines retained their earlier glamour, but where cold economic realities made sheer wealth more important than inner nobility.

Beyond her social symbolism, Tess represents fallen humanity in a religious sense, as the frequent biblical allusions in the novel remind us. Just as Tess's clan was once glorious and powerful but is now sadly diminished, so too did the early glory of the first humans, Adam and Eve, fade with their expulsion from Eden, making humans sad shadows of what they once were. Tess thus represents what is known in Christian theology as *original sin,* the degraded state in which all humans live, even when—like Tess herself after killing Prince or succumbing to Alec—they are not wholly or directly responsible for the sins for which they are punished. This torment represents the most universal side of Tess: she is the myth of the human who suffers for crimes that are not her own and lives a life more degraded than she deserves.

ALEC D'URBERVILLE

An insouciant twenty-four-year-old man, heir to a fortune, and bearer of a name that his father purchased, Alec is the nemesis and downfall of Tess's life. His first name, Alexander, suggests the con-queror—as in Alexander the Great—who seizes what he wants regardless of moral propriety. Yet he is more slippery than a grand conqueror. His full last name, Stoke-d'Urberville, symbolizes the split character of his family, whose origins are simpler than their pretensions to grandeur. After all, Stokes is a blunt and inelegant name. Indeed, the divided and duplicitous character of Alec is evident to the very end of the novel, when he quickly abandons his newfound Christian faith upon remeeting Tess. It is hard to believe Alec holds his religion, or anything else, sincerely. His supposed conversion may only be a new role he is playing.

This duplicity of character is so intense in Alec, and its conse-quences for Tess so severe, that he becomes diabolical. The first part of his surname conjures associations with fiery energies, as in the stoking of a furnace or the flames of hell. His devilish associations are evident when he wields a pitchfork while addressing Tess early in the novel, and when he seduces her as the serpent in Genesis seduced Eve. Additionally, like the famous depiction of Satan in Milton's *Paradise Lost,* Alec does not try to hide his bad qualities. In fact, like Satan, he revels in them. In Chapter XII, he bluntly tells Tess, "I suppose I am a bad fellow—a damn bad fellow. I was born bad, and I have lived bad, and I shall die bad, in all probability." There is frank acceptance in this admission and no shame. Some readers feel Alec is too wicked to be believable, but, like Tess herself, he represents a larger moral principle rather than a real individual man. Like Satan, Alec symbolizes the base forces of life that drive a person away from moral perfection and greatness.

ANGEL CLARE

A freethinking son born into the family of a provincial parson and determined to set himself up as a farmer instead of going to Cambridge like his conformist brothers, Angel represents a rebellious striving toward a personal vision of goodness. He is a secularist who yearns to work for the "honor and glory of man," as he tells his father in Chapter XVIII, rather than for the honor and glory of God in a more distant world. A typical young nineteenth-century progressive, Angel sees human society as a thing to be remolded and improved, and he fervently believes in the nobility of man. He rejects the values handed to him, and sets off in search of his own. His love for Tess, a mere milkmaid and his social inferior, is one expression of his disdain for tradition. This independent spirit contributes to his aura of charisma and general attractiveness that makes him the love object of all the milkmaids with whom he works at Talbothays.

As his name—in French, close to "Bright Angel"—suggests, Angel is not quite of this world, but floats above it in a transcendent sphere of his own. The narrator says that Angel shines rather than burns and that he is closer to the intellectually aloof poet Shelley than to the fleshly and passionate poet Byron. His love for Tess may be abstract, as we guess when he calls her "Daughter of Nature" or "Demeter." Tess may be more an archetype or ideal to him than a flesh and blood woman with a complicated life. Angel's ideals of human purity are too elevated to be applied to actual people: Mrs. Durbeyfield's easygoing moral beliefs are much more easily accommodated to real lives such as Tess's. Angel awakens to the actual complexities of real-world morality after his failure in Brazil, and only then he realizes he has been unfair to Tess. His moral system is readjusted as he is brought down to Earth. Ironically, it is not the angel who guides the human in this novel, but the human who instructs the angel, although at the cost of her own life.

THEMES, MOTIFS & SYMBOLS

THEMES

Themes are the fundamental and often universal ideas explored in a literary work.

THE INJUSTICE OF EXISTENCE

Unfairness dominates the lives of Tess and her family to such an extent that it begins to seem like a general aspect of human existence in *Tess of the d'Urbervilles*. Tess does not mean to kill Prince, but she is punished anyway, just as she is unfairly punished for her own rape by Alec. Nor is there justice waiting in heaven. Christianity teaches that there is compensation in the afterlife for unhappiness suffered in this life, but the only devout Christian encountered in the novel may be the reverend, Mr. Clare, who seems more or less content in his life anyway. For others in their misery, Christianity offers little solace of heavenly justice. Mrs. Durbeyfield never mentions otherworldly rewards. The converted Alec preaches heavenly justice for earthly sinners, but his faith seems shallow and insincere. Generally, the moral atmosphere of the novel is not Christian justice at all, but pagan injustice. The forces that rule human life are absolutely unpredictable and not necessarily well-disposed to us. The pre-Christian rituals practiced by the farm workers at the opening of the novel, and Tess's final rest at Stonehenge at the end, remind us of a world where the gods are not just and fair, but whimsical and uncaring. When the narrator concludes the novel with the statement that "'Justice' was done, and the President of the Immortals (in the Aeschylean phrase) had ended his sport with Tess," we are reminded that justice must be put in ironic quotation marks, since it is not really just at all. What passes for "Justice" is in fact one of the pagan gods enjoying a bit of "sport," or a frivolous game.

CHANGING IDEAS OF SOCIAL CLASS
IN VICTORIAN ENGLAND

Tess of the d'Urbervilles presents complex pictures of both the importance of social class in nineteenth-century England and the difficulty of defining class in any simple way. Certainly the Durbeyfields are a powerful emblem of the way in which class is no longer evaluated in Victorian times as it would have been in the Middle Ages—that is, by blood alone, with no attention paid to fortune or worldly success. Indubitably the Durbeyfields have purity of blood, yet for the parson and nearly everyone else in the novel, this fact amounts to nothing more than a piece of genealogical trivia. In the Victorian context, cash matters more than lineage, which explains how Simon Stokes, Alec's father, was smoothly able to use his large fortune to purchase a lustrous family name and transform his clan into the Stoke-d'Urbervilles. The d'Urbervilles pass for what the Durbeyfields truly are—authentic nobility—simply because definitions of class have changed. The issue of class confusion even affects the Clare clan, whose most promising son, Angel, is intent on becoming a farmer and marrying a milkmaid, thus bypassing the traditional privileges of a Cambridge education and a parsonage. His willingness to work side by side with the farm laborers helps endear him to Tess, and their acquaintance would not have been possible if he were a more traditional and elitist aristocrat. Thus, the three main characters in the Angel-Tess-Alec triangle are all strongly marked by confusion regarding their respective social classes, an issue that is one of the main concerns of the novel.

MEN DOMINATING WOMEN

One of the recurrent themes of the novel is the way in which men can dominate women, exerting a power over them linked primarily to their maleness. Sometimes this command is purposeful, in the man's full knowledge of his exploitation, as when Alec acknowledges how bad he is for seducing Tess for his own momentary pleasure. Alec's act of abuse, the most life-altering event that Tess experiences in the novel, is clearly the most serious instance of male domination over a female. But there are other, less blatant examples of women's passivity toward dominant men. When, after Angel reveals that he prefers Tess, Tess's friend Retty attempts suicide and her friend Marian becomes an alcoholic, which makes their earlier schoolgirl-type crushes on Angel seem disturbing. This devotion is not merely fanciful love, but unhealthy obsession. These girls appear utterly dominated by a desire for a man who, we are told explicitly, does not even realize that they are interested in him. This sort of unconscious male domination of women is perhaps even more unsettling than Alec's outward and self-conscious cruelty.

Even Angel's love for Tess, as pure and gentle as it seems, dominates her in an unhealthy way. Angel substitutes an idealized picture of Tess's country purity for the real-life woman that he continually refuses to get to know. When Angel calls Tess names like "Daughter of Nature" and "Artemis," we feel that he may be denying her true self in favor of a mental image that he prefers. Thus, her identity and experiences are suppressed, albeit unknowingly. This pattern of male domination is finally reversed with Tess's murder of Alec, in which, for the first time in the novel, a woman takes active steps against a man. Of course, this act only leads to even greater suppression of a woman by men, when the crowd of male police officers arrest Tess at Stonehenge. Nevertheless, for just a moment, the accepted pattern of submissive women bowing to dominant men is interrupted, and Tess's act seems heroic.

MOTIFS

Motifs are recurring structures, contrasts, or literary devices that can help to develop and inform the text's major themes.

BIRDS
Images of birds recur throughout the novel, evoking or contradicting their traditional spiritual association with a higher realm of transcendence. Both the Christian dove of peace and the Romantic songbirds of Keats and Shelley, which symbolize sublime heights, lead us to expect that birds will have positive meaning in this novel. Tess occasionally hears birdcalls on her frequent hikes across the countryside; their free expressiveness stands in stark contrast to Tess's silent and constrained existence as a wronged and disgraced girl. When Tess goes to work for Mrs. d'Urberville, she is surprised to find that the old woman's pet finches are frequently released to fly free throughout the room. These birds offer images of hope and liberation. Yet there is irony attached to birds as well, making us doubt whether these images of hope and freedom are illusory. Mrs. d'Urberville's birds leave little white spots on the upholstery, which presumably some servant—perhaps Tess herself—will have to clean. It may be that freedom for one creature entails hardship for another,

just as Alec's free enjoyment of Tess's body leads her to a lifetime of
suffering. In the end, when Tess encounters the pheasants maimed
by hunters and lying in agony, birds no longer seem free, but rather
oppressed and submissive. These pheasants are no Romantic songbirds hovering far above the Earth—they are victims of earthly violence, condemned to suffer down below and never fly again.

THE BOOK OF GENESIS

The Genesis story of Adam and Eve in the Garden of Eden is evoked
repeatedly throughout *Tess of the d'Urbervilles,* giving the novel a
broader metaphysical and philosophical dimension. The roles of
Eve and the serpent in paradise are clearly delineated: Angel is the
noble Adam newly born, while Tess is the indecisive and troubled
Eve. When Tess gazes upon Angel in Chapter XXVII, "she regarded
him as Eve at her second waking might have regarded Adam." Alec,
with his open avowal that he is bad to the bone, is the conniving
Satan. He seduces Tess under a tree, giving her sexual knowledge in
return for her lost innocence. The very name of the forest where this
seduction occurs, the Chase, suggests how Eve will be chased from
Eden for her sins. This guilt, which will never be erased, is known in
Christian theology as the original sin that all humans have inher-
ited. Just as John Durbeyfield is told in Chapter I that "you don't
live anywhere," and his family is evicted after his death at the end of
the novel, their homelessness evokes the human exile from Eden.
Original sin suggests that humans have fallen from their once great
status to a lower station in life, just as the d'Urbervilles have
devolved into the modern Durbeyfields. This Story of the Fall—or
of the "Pure Drop," to recall the name of a pub in Tess's home village—is much more than a social fall. It is an explanation of how all
of us humans—not only Tess—never quite seem to live up to our
expectations, and are never able to inhabit the places of grandeur
we feel we deserve.

VARIANT NAMES

The transformation of the d'Urbervilles into the Durbeyfields is one
example of the common phenomenon of renaming, or variant nam-
ing, in the novel. Names matter in this novel. Tess knows and
accepts that she is a lowly Durbeyfield, but part of her still believes,
as her parents also believe, that her aristocratic original name
should be restored. John Durbeyfield goes a step further than Tess,
and actually renames himself Sir John, as his tombstone epitaph

shows. Another character who renames himself is Simon Stokes, Angel's father, who purchased a family tree and made himself Simon Stoke-d'Urberville. The question raised by all these cases of name changing, whether successful or merely imagined, is the extent to which an altered name brings with it an altered identity. Alec acts notoriously ungentlemanly throughout the novel, but by the end, when he appears at the d'Urberville family vault, his lordly and commanding bearing make him seem almost deserving of the name his father has bought, like a spoiled medieval nobleman. Hardy's interest in name changes makes reality itself seem changeable according to whims of human perspective. The village of Blakemore, as we are reminded twice in Chapters I and II, is also known as Blackmoor, and indeed Hardy famously renames the southern English countryside as "Wessex." He imposes a fictional map on a real place, with names altered correspondingly. Reality may not be as solid as the names people confer upon it.

SYMBOLS

Symbols are objects, characters, figures, or colors used to represent abstract ideas or concepts.

PRINCE

When Tess dozes off in the wagon and loses control, the resulting death of the Durbeyfield horse, Prince, spurs Tess to seek aid from the d'Urbervilles, setting the events of the novel in motion. The horse's demise is thus a powerful plot motivator, and its name a potent symbol of Tess's own claims to aristocracy. Like the horse, Tess herself bears a high-class name, but is doomed to a lowly life of physical labor. Interestingly, Prince's death occurs right after Tess dreams of ancient knights, having just heard the news that her family is aristocratic. Moreover, the horse is pierced by the forward-jutting piece of metal on a mail coach, which is reminiscent of a wound one might receive in a medieval joust. In an odd way, Tess's dream of medieval glory comes true, and her horse dies a heroic death. Yet her dream of meeting a prince while she kills her own Prince, and with him her family's only means of financial sustenance, is a tragic foreshadowing of her own story. The death of the horse symbolizes the sacrifice of real-world goods, such as a useful animal or even her own honor, through excessive fantasizing about a better world.

THE D'URBERVILLE FAMILY VAULT

A double-edged symbol of both the majestic grandeur and the lifeless hollowness of the aristocratic family name that the Durbeyfields learn they possess, the d'Urberville family vault represents both the glory of life and the end of life. Since Tess herself moves from passivity to active murder by the end of the novel, attaining a kind of personal grandeur even as she brings death to others and to herself, the double symbolism of the vault makes it a powerful site for the culminating meeting between Alec and Tess. Alec brings Tess both his lofty name and, indirectly, her own death later; it is natural that he meets her in the vault in d'Urberville Aisle, where she reads her own name inscribed in stone and feels the presence of death. Yet the vault that sounds so glamorous when rhapsodized over by John Durbeyfield in Chapter I seems, by the end, strangely hollow and meaningless. When Alec stomps on the floor of the vault, it produces only a hollow echo, as if its basic emptiness is a complement to its visual grandeur. When Tess is executed, her ancestors are said to snooze on in their crypts, as if uncaring even about the fate of a member of their own majestic family. Perhaps the secret of the family crypt is that its grandiosity is ultimately meaningless.

BRAZIL

Rather surprising for a novel that seems set so solidly in rural England, the narration shifts very briefly to Brazil when Angel takes leave of Tess and heads off to establish a career in farming. Even more exotic for a Victorian English reader than America or Australia, Brazil is the country in which Robinson Crusoe made his fortune and it seems to promise a better life far from the humdrum familiar world. Brazil is thus more than a geographical entity on the map in this novel: it symbolizes a fantasyland, a place where dreams come true. As Angel's name suggests, he is a lofty visionary who lacks some experience with the real world, despite all his mechanical know-how in farm management. He may be able to milk cows, but he does not yet know how to tell the difference between an exotic dream and an everyday reality, so inevitably his experience in the imagined dream world of Brazil is a disaster that he barely survives. His fiasco teaches him that ideals do not exist in life, and this lesson helps him reevaluate his disappointment with Tess's imperfections, her failure to incarnate the ideal he expected her to be. For Angel, Brazil symbolizes the impossibility of ideals, but also forgiveness and acceptance of life in spite of those disappointed ideals.

Summary & Analysis

Phase the First: The Maiden, Chapters I–III

Summary: Chapter I

> *"Don't you really know, Durbeyfield, that you are the lineal representative of the ancient and knightly family of the d'Urbervilles . . . ?"* (See QUOTATIONS, p. 55)

On his way home to the village of Marlott, a middle-aged peddler named John Durbeyfield encounters an old parson who surprises him by addressing him as "Sir John." The old man, Parson Tringham, claims to be a student of history and says that he recently came across a record indicating that Durbeyfield descends from a noble family, the d'Urbervilles. Tringham says that Durbeyfield's noble roots come from so far back in history that they are meaningless, but Durbeyfield becomes quite self-important following the discovery and sends for a horse and carriage to carry him home.

Summary: Chapter II

At the same moment, Durbeyfield's daughter Tess enjoys the May Day festivities with the other women from her village. Durbeyfield rides by in the carriage, and though Tess is embarrassed at the spectacle, she defends her father from the mockery of the other girls. The group goes to the village green for dancing, where they meet three highborn brothers. Tess notices one of the brothers in particular, a young man named Angel Clare. While his two brothers want to keep traveling, Angel cannot pass up the opportunity to dance with these women. The girls ask him to choose his partner, and he chooses a girl other than Tess. They dance for a short time, and then Angel leaves, realizing he must catch up with his determined brothers. Upon leaving, Angel notices Tess and regrets his decision to dance with someone else.

SUMMARY: CHAPTER III

When Tess returns home, she receives a twofold alarm from her mother, Joan, who tells her that her father comes from noble lineage and also that he has been diagnosed with a serious heart condition. Mrs. Durbeyfield has consulted the *Compleat Fortune-Teller,* a large, old book, for guidance. A believer in such astrology, she keeps the book hidden in the outhouse out of an irrational fear of keeping it indoors.

Mr. Durbeyfield is not home, but is instead at Rolliver's, the local inn and drinking establishment, probably taking the opportunity to celebrate his newly discovered heritage. Tess and the family are not surprised to hear of his whereabouts. Tess's mother goes to fetch her husband from the inn but does not return. The narrator explains that her failure to return may result from Mrs. Durbeyfield's enjoyment in sitting at Rolliver's with her husband, since it is time that they can share alone. Tess becomes worried and asks her little brother Abraham to go to Rolliver's and see what is taking their mother and father so long to return. Sometime later, when still no one has returned home, Tess goes after them herself.

ANALYSIS: CHAPTERS I–III

Tess of the d'Urbervilles begins with a rich, lavish description of the landscape that provides the setting of the novel. This description helps establish the context and feel of the story that is to follow. The novel is set in Wessex, a rustic and historical part of southwestern England that relies heavily on farming. This area, as we see it, has its own distinct customs, rituals, beliefs, and culture, and its inhabitants speak with a noticeable rural accent. Hardy became well known for the richly detailed description in his novels, which serves an important function: as Hardy documents and includes many realistic details to present the area more fully, he enables us to enter into the story ourselves in a more concrete and richly imagined way.

We are introduced to the Durbeyfield family on the day in which the legend of their distant, defunct, yet still marvelous aristocratic heritage is revealed. When told of this legacy, Mr. Durbeyfield feels immediately liberated from his poverty and low social stature, even though his situation does not change. Mr. Durbeyfield has already become enraptured in a dream that takes him from rags to riches. Similarly, we first meet Tess at an event that marks a holiday from her everyday life. At the May Day dance, all the young women dress in white, carry white willow branches and white flowers, and dance with each other. This local custom is, at its root, a symbolic ritual of purity and springtime. These women seem to enjoy the custom, perhaps because it allows them the chance to play a symbolic function beyond their insignificant social roles. The arrival of the three young brothers excites the women, heightening the specialness of the affair. When Angel stops to dance with one of them, it is as if he is a prince who has come in search of a princess, even if only for a dance. Most of the women, including Tess, are anxious to be chosen, and somewhat jealous when they are not. Acceptance from a handsome man from a higher social class would mean a lot to them. Like Mr. Durbeyfield, these young local women yearn to escape poverty and the low social stature that their rural setting allots to them.

Mrs. Durbeyfield's belief in superstitions and her trust in her fortune-telling book also demonstrate a strong, perhaps irrational hope in what the future holds. She believes that something good is meant to happen to her and her family and that it is only a matter of time until it does. Through all of these characters and actions we are introduced to the concept of fate, or a belief in a predetermined, unavoidable future. Ironically, Tess's parents' blind faith in their ability to climb the social hierarchy leads them to make costly decisions later in the novel. The news about their ancestry seems to augur a hopeful change in their fortunes, but it is really just an instrument in the catastrophe that fate brings about.

CHAPTERS IV–VII

SUMMARY: CHAPTER IV

At the inn, Tess's young brother Abraham overhears Mr. and Mrs. Durbeyfield discussing their plans for Tess to take the news of her ancestry to the wealthy Mrs. d'Urberville in the hopes that she will make Tess's fortune. When Tess arrives, she realizes her father will probably be too tired and drunk to take his load of beehives to the market in a few hours. Her prediction comes true, so she and her brother Abraham deliver them instead. On the way, Abraham tells Tess of their parents' plans, and then the conversation veers onto the topic of astronomy. Knowing that stars contain clusters of worlds like their own, Abraham asks Tess if those worlds are better or worse than the world in which they live. Tess boldly answers that other stars are better and that their star is a "blighted one." Tess explains that this shortcoming is the reason for all of her and her family's misfortunes.

Abraham falls asleep, leaving Tess to contemplate. She too eventually falls asleep and dreams about a "gentlemanly suitor" who grimaces and laughs at her. Suddenly, Tess and Abraham are awakened by a calamity. Their carriage has collided with the local mail cart, and the collision has killed Prince, their old horse. Realizing that the loss of their horse will be economically devastating for her family, Tess is overcome with guilt. The surrounding foliage seems to turn pale and white as Tess does. The carriage is hitched up to the wagon of a local farmer, who helps them bring the beehives toward the market in Casterbridge.

Later, Tess returns home ashamed, but no one blames Tess more than she does herself. Tess remains the only one who recognizes the impact that the loss of the horse will have. The farmer helps them return Prince's body back to the Durbeyfield's home. Refusing to scrap or sell the body, Mr. Durbeyfield labors harder than he has in an entire month to bury his beloved horse.

Summary: Chapter V
In part because of her guilt over the horse, Tess agrees with her mother's plan to send her to Mrs. d'Urberville. When she arrives, she does not find the crumbling old mansion she expects, but rather a new and fashionable home. She meets Mrs. d'Urberville's son Alec, who, captivated by Tess's beauty, agrees to try to help her. Alec says that his mother is unwell, but he says he will see what he can do for Tess.

Summary: Chapter VI
When Tess returns home, she finds a letter. It is from Mrs. d'Urberville, offering her a job tending the d'Urbervilles' fowls. Tess looks for other jobs closer to home, but she cannot find anything. Hoping to earn enough money to buy a new horse for her family, Tess accepts the d'Urbervilles' job and decides to go back to Trantridge.

Summary: Chapter VII
On the day Tess is scheduled to leave for the d'Urbervilles' home, Mrs. Durbeyfield cajoles her into wearing her best clothes. Mrs. Durbeyfield dresses Tess up and is pleased by her own efforts, as is Mr. Durbeyfield, who begins speculating about a price at which he will sell their family title. When Alec arrives to retrieve Tess, they

become uncertain that she is doing the right t'
as does Mrs. Durbeyfield, who worries that
advantage of her daughter.

ANALYSIS: CHAPTERS IV–VII

Tess of the d'Urbervilles is rich in sy
noticeable in as Tess drives the wagon in Chap
dream about a man of nobility who stands laughing at her a
ing down on her plight. Tess wakes up to realize that she has literally
killed her Prince, the family's horse, and along with it the family's
means of support. Symbolically, the inability of the Durbeyfields to
deliver the load of beehives mirrors their inability to transcend their
social class. Even with the knowledge of their supposed noble heritage, without physical productivity, the calamities that befall them
in the present stunt the Durbeyfields' dreams of future social mobi-
lization and other lofty goals. The novel thus prioritizes work and
contribution over nobility and entitlement. As Prince's death immo-
bilizes their only marketable good, the Durbeyfields must suffer the
tragedy that lies ahead.

Tess of the d'Urbervilles follows a simple but carefully con-
structed pattern. Hardy establishes a set of basic plot mechanisms
that govern the structure of his story and employs them without
drastic variation. The novel is divided into seven phases, each of
which tells a concise and particular story within the larger story of
Tess's life, and accomplishes some specific goals in moving Tess
from her simple country life to her tragic circumstances at the end of
her life. These chapters successively show Tess's development into a
responsible young adult. The responsibility she feels for the death of
Prince compels her to pay her family back. This guilt leads her to
visit the d'Urbervilles and puts her into an uncertain and potentially
dangerous situation. These chapters also mark the beginning of her
downfall, as she blindly offers to work at Trantridge for the sake of
her family.

Though it is early in the novel, distinct pictures of each of the
characters already start to emerge. We can see Tess's highly developed sense of responsibility as she answers her brother Abraham's
questions and completes the work neglected by her parents. Tess's
beauty and nobility of character are also emphasized, as are her
strong conscience and sense of familial duty. Mr. and Mrs. Durbeyfield's weaknesses—his laziness and her simplemindedness—add a

urgency to Tess's family responsibilities. If not for Tess, rbeyfields might be very badly off indeed. Alec is obviously vious and opportunistic, an impression reinforced in every ene in which he appears. He is repeatedly associated with darkness and dark colors, reflecting the shadiness of his own character. From his first meeting with Tess, he behaves awkwardly and inappropriately, addressing her with intimate nicknames like "my pretty coz." Alec's unappealing traits are easily recognizable. To an extent, at this point in the novel the characters seem somewhat one-dimensional. Even Angel Clare, who appears only briefly in this section, is portrayed as graceful, kind, and life-loving, presaging what we see of him later. But at the same time, by giving us a strong sense of these characters and what kinds of things they are likely to do, Hardy is able to generate a great deal of suspense, drawing us into his plots of seduction, betrayal, and loyalty. Moreover, the changes that we see later in the novel seem momentous, surprising, and important after this vivid beginning.

CHAPTERS VIII–XI

SUMMARY: CHAPTER VIII

On the way to the d'Urberville estate, Alec drives recklessly, and Tess pleads with him to stop. He continues at a fast pace and tells her to hold on to his waist. She complies only out of fear for her safety. When traveling down the next steep hill, he urges her to hold on to him again, but she refuses and pleads with him to slow down. He agrees to drive more slowly, but only if she will allow him to kiss her. Tess allows him to kiss her on the cheek, but when she unthinkingly wipes the kiss off with her handkerchief, he becomes angry and outraged at her unwillingness to submit to his advances. They argue, and Tess finishes the journey on foot.

SUMMARY: CHAPTER IX

The next morning Tess meets Mrs. d'Urberville for the first time and discovers that the old woman is blind. Tess is surprised by Mrs. d'Urberville's lack of appreciation for Tess's coming to work for her. Mrs. d'Urberville asks Tess to place each of the fowls on her lap so she can examine and pet them. She tells Tess to whistle to her bullfinches every morning. Tess agrees and leaves. Tess is later unable to blow any whistles, and Alec agrees to help her remember how.

SUMMARY: CHAPTER X

After several weeks at the d'Urbervilles', Tess goes to the market. Tess has not frequented this market very often, but realizes that she likes it and plans to make future returns. Several months later, she goes to the market and discovers that her visit has coincided with a local fair. That evening, she waits for some friends to walk her home and declines Alec's offer to take her himself. When her friends are ready to leave, Tess finds that some of them are drunk, and they express their irritation that she has Alec's attention all to herself. The scene grows unpleasant. Suddenly Alec arrives on his horse, and Tess finally agrees to let him carry her away.

SUMMARY: CHAPTER XI

Alec lets the horse wander off the path and deep into the woods, where he tries to convince Tess to take him as a lover. Tess is reticent, and Alec realizes that they have become lost in the fog. He gives Tess his coat and goes to look for a landmark. Still trying to win her favor as a lover, he tells Tess that he has bought her father a new horse. When he returns, Tess is asleep, and Alec uses the opportunity to take advantage of her sexually.

ANALYSIS: CHAPTERS VIII–XI

These chapters mark the second half of Phase the First, which is subtitled "The Maiden," and establishes several of the major characters. Structurally, the main plot follows a linear progression, depicting the direct progress of Tess's life from the time her father learns of their noble heritage to her falling prey to Alec d'Urberville's advances. This event is truly a catastrophe for her, because in Victorian England any kind of sexual encounter would earn a young woman moral rebuke and social condemnation, regardless of how the man involved conducted himself. In a way, Tess's fall can be seen as a direct result of her father's discovery of their noble descent. Tess is sent to take advantage of the familial connection, but instead, Alec takes advantage of her.

The plot hinges on a great many unfortunate coincidences, including Simon Stokes's fortuitous decision to call himself "d'Urberville," the accidental death of old Prince, and Tess's bad luck in being held up with her drunken friends after the fair. Throughout the novel, many events actually hinge on improbable coincidences. Hardy uses this technique to convey the sense that the universe itself, in the guise of fate, opposes Tess and foreordains her tragedy. Some critics, however, have accused these coincidences of straining the bounds of credulity, making the novel less believable.

With the plot mechanics so neatly worked out, Hardy is able to spend a great deal of time creating his world; indeed, one of the novel's strongest characteristics is its evocation of landscape and scenery. The Vale of Blackmoor, where the novel is set, is presented as a kind of lovely rustic ideal, where the atmosphere "is so tinged with azure that what artists call the middle distance partakes also of that hue, while the horizon beyond is of the deepest ultramarine." It is a place also where the weather and atmosphere tend to adapt to the action of the story, especially when the confusing, disorienting, eerie shrouds of mist cloak the forest on the night of Tess's fall.

The imagery of mist and shadows mirrors Tess's inner landscape, reflecting her own confusion and insecurity. This setting also reflects the mystery within which Hardy cloaks what actually happens to Tess that night. Hardy never reveals the specific details that would enable us to decide for ourselves whether Tess is a willing participant or a victim of rape. Hardy's narrator does not seem to care about this distinction: the narrator describes Alec's actions as ruthless, unjust, and coarse, whatever the details, but he does not judge Tess at all. This portrayal of Tess's fall may have struck Hardy's original readers as scandalous, since Victorian society would have tended toward the opposite perspective, judging the woman more harshly than the man, regardless of the circumstances. But the narrator avoids commenting on Tess's behavior by remarking that her disgrace is simply meant to be—it is fated, and is part of the way of the world. If Tess's misfortune is truly predestined, she is not responsible for it, and she cannot really be judged as good or bad. This conundrum is typical of Hardy—he makes us care deeply about Tess, inviting us to think carefully about the morality and practical wisdom of her decisions, and then shocks us by pronouncing sagely that all of these moral considerations are irrelevant. Even when Tess tries hardest to be good, her bad luck conspires to get her into trouble, as when her virtuous unwillingness to partake in the festivities makes her more susceptible to Alec's depredations.

PHASE THE SECOND:
MAIDEN NO MORE, CHAPTERS XII–XV

SUMMARY: CHAPTER XII

After a few weeks of confused dalliance with Alec, Tess realizes she feels no love for him, and decides to flee from the d'Urberville mansion to her home during the early morning hours. Alec discovers her on the road, questions her early departure, and tries to convince her to return with him. When she refuses, he offers to drive her the rest of the way home, but she refuses even this offer. Alec tells Tess to let him know should she ever need help.

Tess continues on her way home, randomly passing by a sign painter who is busy painting Bible passages onto random walls and gates throughout the countryside. He interrupts his conversation with Tess to paint a sign, which says "THY DAMNATION SLUMBERETH NOT." These words resound in Tess's mind, and she asks the painter if he believes the words he paints. He answers affirmatively. She tries to ask him for advice about her plight, but he tells her to go see a clergyman at a nearby church. She continues home, where her mother is surprised to see her. Her mother is frustrated with her for refusing to marry Alec, but she softens when Tess reminds her mother that she never warned Tess of the danger she faced.

SUMMARY: CHAPTER XIII

Some of Tess's friends come to visit, and in their high-spirited company Tess feels cheered. But in the morning she lapses back into her depression: to her, the future seems endless and bleak. She tries to attend church but hears the crowd whispering about her. Shaken, she falls into the habit of only going out after dark.

SUMMARY: CHAPTER XIV

The following August, Tess decides the time has come to stop pitying herself, and she helps her village with the harvest. Her baby boy, conceived with Alec, falls ill, and Tess becomes worried that he will die without a proper christening. She decides to christen him herself and names him Sorrow. When he dies the following morning, Tess asks the parson if her christening was sufficient to earn her baby a Christian burial. Moved, the parson replies that though he cannot bury the child himself, Tess may do so. That night Tess lays Sorrow to rest in a corner of the churchyard, and makes a little cross for his grave.

SUMMARY: CHAPTER XV

Tess realizes she can never be happy in Marlott and longs to begin a new life in a place where her past is unknown. The next year, the chance arises for Tess to become a milkmaid at the Talbothays Dairy. She seizes the opportunity, in part drawn by the fact that the dairy lies near the ancestral estate of the d'Urbervilles and spurred on by "the invincible instinct towards self-delight."

ANALYSIS: CHAPTERS XII–XV

Phase the Second, subtitled "Maiden No More," lays out the consequences of Tess's fall in Phase the First. Tess flees Trantridge, pledging violence to Alec in an uncharacteristic manner, which proves that she does not remain complicit with fate and instead promises to be proactive in changing it. At home, she incurs her mother's disappointment, fueling the need to fulfill her familial obligations. Later, she bears her doomed son Sorrow and buries him, against the precepts of the church and proper society. She is miserably unhappy throughout this period, but her unhappiness seems to stem at least as much from her fall from the grace of society and from her own troubled conscience as from her child's birth and death, which are treated almost tangentially. Tess is sad when he dies, but she seems just as upset when villagers whisper about her in church—she even begins shunning daylight to avoid prying eyes. Tess's early one-sidedness gives way to an identity crisis in which she is torn apart by her hatred of Alec, her guilt toward her family, her shame within society, and her disappointment in herself.

However we view Tess's struggle with what has happened to her, we are likely to consider her an innocent victim and to be sufficiently impressed with her character that we react with outrage to her unhappy fate. As she asks her mother, "How could I be expected to know? I was a child when I left this house four months ago. Why didn't you tell me there was danger in men-folk? Why didn't you warn me?" Tess sees herself as a victim of her own ignorance. She can claim that she did not know the dangers a man such as Alec d'Urberville posed and that it is not fair that she is made to suffer for succumbing to an unknown danger. When Tess refuses to marry Alec despite the social advantage the match would give her, and refuses his offers of help because she does not sincerely love him, we see her as more than an unwitting victim: her integrity and courage make her heroic.

Phase the Second is primarily a transitional period, taking Tess from the scene of her disgrace to the promise of a new life at Talbothays. But it also begins to crystallize some important themes in the novel. We see in the previous section that Tess is fated to tragedy. In this section, we learn about the human instinct that leads Tess to oppose her fate, "the invincible instinct towards self-delight." Tess's healthy desire simply to be happy is perhaps the source of her great courage and moral strength. Additionally, the novel's exploration of nobility, which begins with Mr. Durbeyfield's discovery of his aristocratic heritage, is developed further here. In the previous section, the upper-class Alec trifles shamelessly with the lower-class Tess. With Tess's moral integrity shown to its fullest extent, we begin to see Tess as truly noble through her goodness and her determination. Of course, the irony is that Tess is actually the real possessor of the d'Urberville name, while Alec is simply an imposter, the amoral son of a merchant and, hence, a commoner.

PHASE THE THIRD: THE RALLY, CHAPTERS XVI–XIX

SUMMARY: CHAPTER XVI
In good spirits, Tess sets out to begin work at the Talbothays Dairy, located in the Valley of the Great Dairies. On her way, the new scenery enchants her as she travels through the mists of Blackmoor. The beautiful day and the beautiful landscape put Tess in an optimistic mood. She passes the burial ground of her ancient ancestors, but decides to keep going.

SUMMARY: CHAPTER XVII
Tess finally arrives at the Talbothays Dairy. Richard Crick, the master dairyman, treats her kindly and offers to let her rest, but she prefers to begin work immediately. She quickly fits in and feels very much at home. One of the men at the dairy looks familiar to her, and she recognizes him as the highbrow man whom she noticed back at the May Day village dance in Marlott. That evening, Tess overhears the dairymaids talking about him and learns that he is Angel Clare, the son of a well-respected Wessex clergyman. Angel's two brothers have also joined the church, but Angel himself prefers a life in agriculture and, thus, has come to the dairy to learn about its work.

There is much talk about Angel among the other dairymaids, and many of them seem to have a crush on him.

SUMMARY: CHAPTER XVIII

The narrator shifts away from Tess's point of view to tell us Angel's background story. Angel is the most gifted of the three brothers, but, because his father looked upon a university education solely as preparation for a clerical life, Angel decided not to go to Cambridge. He has doubts about the doctrines of the church and feels that it would be dishonest to join the clergy. He has spent time in London in an attempt to find a business profession and has been involved with an older woman. Finally, he decided that the life of the soil would enable him to preserve his intellectual liberty outside the stifling conditions of city life. Now twenty-six years old, he learns firsthand about farming by visiting sites devoted to the subject. He is gentlemanly and thoughtful and is treated as a superior by most of the workers at the dairy. Angel acts aloof and a bit shy at first, but he soon befriends the other workers and spends more time with them. He swiftly finds himself drawn to Tess's beauty and thinks that she seems uncommonly virginal and pure. Tess, however, tries to stay away from him out of shame for her secret, woeful past.

SUMMARY: CHAPTER XIX

After a few weeks, Tess discovers that Angel is breaking the dairy's rules by lining up her favorite cows for her. She tells him of her discovery and, later that night, walks alone in the garden, listening to him strum his harp. He comes down to join her, and they have an intimate conversation. Angel finds it compelling that a girl as young and beautiful as Tess would have such a dark view of life. She deflects his questions about her with general comments about life, and then she inquires about him. Tess is interested in Angel's education and learning, and she also wonders why such a well-bred and well-schooled man would choose to become a farmer instead of joining his father and brothers in the clergy. He offers to tutor her, but she refuses, claiming that the answers she seeks are not to be found in books.

ANALYSIS: CHAPTERS XVI–XIX

These chapters portray the beginning of the happiest period of Tess's life. The narrator indicates that she "had never been in her recent life so happy as she was now, possibly never would be so happy again." This turn in tone is matched by a healthier landscape, and she is perfectly suited to her surroundings. Tess's simple, rustic beauty is matched by the country paradise of the dairy, and the ripening weather of summer matches the blossoming romance between Tess and Angel.

Tess is in control of her emotions and, it appears, of her life. The setting allows her to deal with her past melancholy, and these chapters serve as development, on a number of levels, of Tess's newfound success: her return to normal life, her achievement as a worker, and her success as a more virtuous lover. This perspective is mirrored by the background of Talbothays, a quiet, slow-paced paradise where Tess can be calm and comfortable.

Tess's assertion that the answers she seeks are not to be found in books indicates that she wants to learn directly from life experiences. Tess is ready to experience the world, and, of course, she has already made some mistakes as a result. Her assertion demonstrates that she wants to become knowledgeable and self-sufficient. In other words, she does not want to rely on anyone else. This independence contrasts with the way Tess's mother used to consult the fortune-telling book for all her guidance. In the same way that Angel seeks to become independent from his family's current legacy, Tess wants to become independent of hers.

These chapters fully introduce Angel into the novel. A great deal of narrative and an entire chapter are devoted to summarizing his recent accomplishments and family background. Given that Angel is introduced immediately after the saga between Tess and the ruthless Alec d'Urberville, the contrasts between these two men emerge vividly in these chapters. For instance, Angel has soothing, elegant conversations with Tess and gives her classical, idealistic nicknames like "Artemis" and "Demeter." Alec, on the other hand, mocks her with demeaning words and low-society nicknames like "coz." Through this juxtaposition, Angel appears an angel and a savior to the troubled but coping Tess.

CHAPTERS XX–XXIV

SUMMARY: CHAPTER XX

As the months pass, Angel and Tess grow closer, and Tess finds herself in the happiest phase of her life. They wake up early, before the others, and feel as if they are the only people on Earth. Indeed, the dairy seems to be an Eden, where Angel is Adam and Tess is Eve. Tess is Angel's "visionary essence of woman," and he playfully nicknames her "Artemis" and "Demeter." Tess does not understand these nicknames and simply tells him to call her Tess. They continue to enjoy the morning, as the summer fog slowly lifts and birds swoop and play in the misty air.

SUMMARY: CHAPTER XXI

Life on the dairy begins to change. There is worry about the butter, which is not churning properly. Mrs. Crick jokes that this sort of thing happens only when someone on the farm falls in love. Indeed, there are two people who are in love, and the milkmaids often discuss Angel's noticeable love for Tess and imagine what the future will hold for them. Tess does not want to marry, though, because she is still ashamed of her past. After some further churning, the butter begins to set and everyone's fears melt away—except for Tess's.

SUMMARY: CHAPTER XXII

Early in the morning, the Cricks receive a letter from a customer who complains that the butter he has bought from them "had a twang," or a sharp taste. Mr. Crick realizes that this taste must be the result of the cows eating from garlic weeds. The dairymaids go out to the pasture to search for these disastrous weeds. Tess feels faint, and Mr. Crick encourages Tess to take a moment to rest. Angel stops with her, and she makes a point of mentioning the virtues of two of her close milkmaid friends, Izz and Retty. Angel agrees that they are nice women and capable dairymaids, but indicates that he has no romantic interest in them.

SUMMARY: CHAPTER XXIII

Two months after her arrival at the dairy, Tess sets out with her friends to attend the Mellstock Church. There has been a torrential downpour the day before, and the girls come to a long stretch of flooded road. Angel offers to carry them across, and they agree. All the girls notice that Angel takes the longest with Tess, and they each realize that he prefers her.

Tess begins to avoid Angel, but she notices from afar his grace and self-discipline in the company of the girls who dote on him. One night, Marian, Izz, and Retty each confess to feeling love for Angel, and Tess feels guilty, since she too loves Angel but has already decided never to marry. She wonders if she is wrong to take so much of his time.

SUMMARY: CHAPTER XXIV
Later that summer, Angel and Tess are milking cows, and Angel is overcome with his feeling for Tess. He embraces her, and she gives way to her feelings for a moment before trying to pull away. Angel tells Tess he loves her and is surprised to hear the words come out of his mouth. No one has noticed their encounter, and the two return to their milking, shaken.

ANALYSIS: CHAPTERS XX–XXIV
These chapters mark the end of Phase the Third, subtitled "The Rally," which concerns Tess's "invincible instinct toward self-delight" as she enjoys a happy period at the Talbothays Dairy and her new romance with Angel Clare. The harsh irony of Angel's first impression of Tess, that she is "virginal," is underplayed by Tess's self-sacrificing virtue throughout these chapters—she even avoids him intentionally when she thinks her friends deserve him more. The plot of this phase is, like that of Phase the First, essentially linear: Tess meets Angel and their relationship grows closer until it becomes clear that he loves her.

A new conflict arises in these chapters between Tess's new love for Angel and her moral reservations about acting on that love. This conflict and indecisiveness on Tess's part is mirrored by the new problems that surface at Talbothays Dairy concerning the quality of the butter. Certain agents have caused the butter to become tainted, affecting its taste and attractiveness. Tess feels a similar inner turmoil with the agents that have affected her, which leads her to think that her attractiveness may be tainted even though Angel expresses his love for her.

With Tess's virtue as uncompromisable as ever, her personal reservations about marrying Angel seem clearly designed to arouse both our sympathy and moral outrage. It seems ludicrous for poor

Tess to have to refrain from acting on her passion. Surely any moral code that would force Tess to suffer for the rest of her life for a single error must be deeply flawed. This line of reasoning is Hardy's argument, but still Tess seems to be fated to suffer, the victim of "the ill-judged execution of the well-judged plan of things."

As Angel and Alec are compared and contrasted in previous chapters, Tess is compared and contrasted with the other dairymaids in these chapters. Tess views herself as equal or subordinate to her friends Marian, Izz, and Retty, but Angel sees her as his sole, perfect mate. All of the dairymaids have crushes on Angel, but Angel is interested only in Tess. The final scene in the section—in which Tess and Angel are overcome by their love—is a wonderful conclusion to these chapters, which have focused on the growing attraction between them. The conclusion satisfies the natural progression of their love in a way that is surely meant to appease us. Tess is surprised by Angel's confession, and a bit shaken by its implications. She is torn because she knows her dark past will stand in the way of her future with Angel, and even as their love continues to grow, these issues and problems do not show any signs of disappearing.

PHASE THE FOURTH: THE CONSEQUENCE, CHAPTERS XXV–XXXI

SUMMARY: CHAPTER XXV

Angel feels that he needs time to understand the nature of his relationship with Tess, so he decides to spend a few days away from the dairy visiting his family. At his father's house in Emminster, he finds his parents breakfasting with his brothers: the Reverend Felix, a town curate, and the Reverend Cuthbert, a college dean at Cambridge. Angel's family notices that his manners have worsened somewhat during his time with common farm folk, while Angel thinks that his brothers have become mentally limited and bogged down by their comfortable situations.

SUMMARY: CHAPTER XXVI

After prayers that evening, Angel and his father discuss Angel's marriage prospects. The Clares hope Angel will marry Mercy Chant, a pious neighbor girl, and they admonish their son about the importance of Christian piety in a wife. Angel contends that a wife who understands farm life would also be an asset, and he tells them about Tess, emphasizing her religious sincerity. The family agrees to meet her. Angel's father also tells Angel that he has saved the money he would have needed for his college education, and, since Angel did not go to college, he is willing to give it to Angel to buy land. Before Angel leaves, his father tells him about his efforts to convert the local populace, and mentions his failed efforts to tame a young miscreant named Alec d'Urberville. Angel's dislike for old families increases.

SUMMARY: CHAPTER XXVII

Angel returns to the dairy, where he finds Tess just awakening from her afternoon nap. He takes her in his arms and asks her to marry him. Tess replies that she loves him but that she cannot marry. Angel replies that he will give her time to think it over, but she replies again that the marriage is impossible. Nevertheless, in the coming days Angel continues to try to persuade her, and Tess quickly realizes that she loves him too strongly to keep up her refusal.

SUMMARY: CHAPTER XXVIII

In the early fall, Angel again asks Tess to marry him. Tess hesitates, saying that one of the other girls might make a better wife than she. Tess still feels that she cannot marry Angel because of the implications of her past indiscretions. But Angel still believes that Tess is objecting only because of her low social status, and he thinks that she will accept soon enough. Tess believes that she must tell Angel about her lineage and her dark past, but hesitates and resolves to tell him later.

SUMMARY: CHAPTER XXIX

The farm floods with gossip about a failed marriage. A man named Jack Dollop married a widow, expecting to partake of her substantial dowry, only to discover that her financial stability and income vanishes as a result of the marriage. Most people at the dairy think the widow was wrong to deceive Jack Dollop of this fact and that she should have been completely truthful with him before marrying. This widespread opinion makes Tess nervous again about her past. She wonders whether she should reveal this past to Angel.

SUMMARY: CHAPTER XXX

As they are taking care of some chores, Angel mentions offhandedly to Tess that they are near the ancestral territory of the ancient d'Urbervilles. She takes the opportunity to tell Angel that she descends from the d'Urbervilles, and he is pleased, realizing that her descent from noble blood will make her a better match in the eyes of his family. At last Tess agrees to marry him, and she begins to weep. Tess asks if she may write to her mother, and when Angel learns she is from Marlott, he remembers where he has seen her before—on May Day, when they did not dance.

SUMMARY: CHAPTER XXXI

When Mrs. Durbeyfield receives Tess's letter, she immediately writes back advising her daughter not to tell Angel about her past. Tess luxuriates throughout October, and, when Angel asks her to finalize the date of their wedding, she again appears reticent, saying she is reluctant to change things. When Angel announces their engagement to Mr. Crick in front of the dairymaids, Tess is impressed by their joyous reaction. She feels that she can finally express her happiness, but she soon feels unworthy of Angel. Tess decides that she will finally tell him about her past.

ANALYSIS: CHAPTERS XXV–XXXI

It is obvious that Angel has become very different from the rest of his family as a result of the time he has spent farming. His brothers have excelled in the ministry and in intellectual circles, and Angel feels that he has nothing in common with them anymore. Overall, Angel's family is somewhat snobbish. They are quite respectable in their religious observances, but they seem to lack the ability to feel and to understand people on an emotional level.

Tess represents many bad things to Mrs. Clare. Angel's mother sees in Tess the beginning of the fall of the great Victorian era of opulence and high society. She does not accept Tess as a suitable daughter-in-law because she believes that Tess will bring down the status of the family. The Clares hope that Angel will find a suitable bride, meaning a highborn, well-bred woman of society. For them, marriage is not about love, but rather social, financial, and religious prosperity. The difference between Angel and the rest of the Clares lies in his progressiveness. He has rejected the clerical profession because he does not believe in serving the church but, rather, working on land and supplying food.

Tess's denial of Angel shows that she is concerned about what her past may mean to her future. To Angel, her denial seems to signify that Tess is even more virtuous than he thought. By denying him not because of a lack of love but, he believes, because of her lack of social status, her convictions seem almost too pure to him. In fact, Angel believes that both his family and Tess suffer from holding onto the belief in a privileged class.

The story of Jack Dollop's wife makes Tess feel nervous again about her predicament. As Angel persistently seeks Tess's acceptance of marriage, Tess continually seeks an opportunity to share her past with him. She understands that a woman's virginity is regarded as supremely important by most of her society, and that Angel does not see her as anything but completely pure. Telling Angel of her family's d'Urberville lineage is difficult enough for her. He takes the news well, but she does not gain confidence that her other, more shameful revelation will be met with the same excitement.

Mrs. Durbeyfield advises Tess against the ethically sound choice of telling Angel about her past. Mrs. Durbeyfield's advice, however, stems from her love and concern for Tess. Like any mother, Mrs. Durbeyfield does not want anything to interfere with her daughter making an advantageous marriage. Tess is relieved to receive this advice from her mother, but she knows deep down that she cannot follow it. Although Tess's mother can advise an unethical course of action in order to preserve her daughter's happiness, Tess's conscience is too strong to live with the secret, and she must free herself of the burden so that she can live comfortably and morally.

CHAPTERS XXXII–XXXIV

SUMMARY: CHAPTER XXXII
Tess agrees to leave the dairy with Angel around Christmas, and their wedding date is set for December 31. Angel hopes to spend that time visiting a flour mill and staying in a home that belonged to the d'Urbervilles. Angel buys Tess clothes for their wedding and, to her relief, quietly takes out a marriage license rather than publicizing his intent to marry Tess.

SUMMARY: CHAPTER XXXIII
While out shopping, Angel and Tess encounter a man from Alec d'Urberville's village, who disparages Tess and denies her virginity. Angel strikes the man, but when the man apologizes, Angel gives him some money. Tess is wracked with guilt, and that night she

writes a confession and slips it under Angel's door. Strangely, in the morning, Angel's behavior toward her has not changed, and he does not mention the letter. Tess ascertains that it slipped under the carpet and that Angel never saw it. On the morning of the wedding, Tess again tries to tell Angel about her past, but he cuts her off, saying that there will be time for such revelations after they are married. The dairyman and his wife accompany them to church, and they are married. As they are leaving for the ceremony, however, a rooster crows in the mid-afternoon.

SUMMARY: CHAPTER XXXIV

After the wedding, the couple travels to the old d'Urberville mansion, where they will have a few days to themselves before the farmer returns. Tess receives a package from Angel's father, containing some jewelry that Angel's godmother bequeathed to his future wife some years ago. The newlyweds enjoy a happy moment, which is broken when the man arrives from the dairy with their luggage, bringing bad news about Tess's friends. After the wedding, Retty attempted suicide and Marian became an alcoholic.

After this disclosure, Angel asks Tess for forgiveness, telling her of his past indiscretion with an older woman in London. Tess says that she, too, has a confession and tells him of her past with Alec.

ANALYSIS: CHAPTERS XXXII–XXXIV

As these chapters mark the end of Phase the Fourth, "The Consequence," they permit the phase to fit well with the seesaw scheme of the novel up to this point. *Tess of the d'Urbervilles* alternates sections that build up to a climax with sections that detail the result of the climax. Phase the First builds steadily toward Tess's fall from grace, and Phase the Second lays out the consequences for Tess—her child and her loss of reputation. Phase the Third builds inexorably toward Tess's union with Angel, while Phase the Fourth brings us the consequences of their love: Angel and Tess marry, and she confesses her past. Aside from the repeated instances of supernatural effect and mystical ill omen, such as the cock crowing in the afternoon and the creaky old mansion, the real conflict in this section is again moral, between Tess's desire to be happily loved by Angel and her conscious obligation to tell him about her past. Because Tess has such a strong instinct for self-delight, she is able to delay and resist her conscience through October. Since Tess has an even stronger sense of moral duty, however, she cannot resist it forever; the section ends as she begins her story, "murmuring the words without flinching, and with her eyelids drooping down."

The universe is still hostile to Tess, and fate still toys with her in the form of the accidental mishaps on which the plot turns. Had Angel received Tess's note before they were married, the course of the story might have gone differently. But the letter happens to slip under the carpet, and another chance for Tess's tragedy to be averted is lost. This fluke may seem like an unbelievable coincidence, except that the universe expresses its hostility toward Tess through the portentous mishaps that plague her throughout the novel. The cock crowing in the afternoon does not doom Tess to ill fortune, but simply announces her foreordained doom to the world.

Indeed, Angel's decision to seek work at Talbothays is one of the most improbable circumstances in the novel. Although we see Angel as a progressive, new-thinking young man, his decision to give up a university education and an esteemed position in the clergy seems almost too idealistic to be true. While we see Tess as the responsible, patient, and persistent character that she is, Angel may appear rather spoiled—the youngest son in a privileged family who is not satisfied with his status quo and seeks adventure in murkier waters. In a sense, Angel is much more childish and naïve than the extremely responsible Tess. Angel may be angelic not in his morality, but in the sense that he is cherubic and childlike, indicating his need to grow and develop a truer love for Tess.

Talbothays Dairy is a kind of classless haven untroubled by social difference. Even Angel, the closest thing Talbothays has to an aristocrat, fits in quite seamlessly. Nevertheless, the themes of social prejudice and noble heritage continue to arise. Angel's mother, who exhibits snobbery throughout the novel, wants Angel to marry a suitable girl—meaning highborn. Angel is pleased to discover Tess's noble background in this section because he knows it will placate his mother, who will conclude that Tess must be worthwhile if she has such a remarkable pedigree. This situation can be interpreted in various ways. On the one hand, it is superficial and reprehensible of Mrs. Clare to place such a high stock in social class. On the other, Tess *is* nobly born, and she *does* possess all the stereotypical characteristics that are supposed to distinguish nobility, such as beauty, courage, and integrity.

PHASE THE FIFTH: THE WOMAN PAYS, CHAPTERS XXXV–XXXIX

SUMMARY: CHAPTER XXXV

Angel is distraught by Tess's confession. He begs her to deny it, but she cannot. He flees the house, and Tess follows after him. For hours, they walk the grounds of the mansion. Tess tells her husband that she will do anything he asks and even offers to drown herself. Angel orders her to go back to the house. When he returns, Tess is asleep. After an uncomfortable moment looking at the d'Urberville ladies' portraits, Angel goes to sleep in a different room.

SUMMARY: CHAPTER XXXVI

Three miserable days go by, during which Angel spends his time at the mill or with his studies. Tess wonders if they should get a divorce, but she learns that the law does not allow divorces. Finally, Tess offers to go home, and Angel tells her she should go.

SUMMARY: CHAPTER XXXVII

> *Clare came close, and bent over her. "Dead, dead,*
> *dead!" he murmured.*   (See QUOTATIONS, p. 56)

That night, Tess wakes up and discovers that Angel is sleepwalking. He stumbles into Tess's room and seizes her in his arms. Moaning that his wife is dead, he carries her over a narrow bridge and into the churchyard, where he lays her in a coffin. Tess carefully leads Angel back into the house, and in the morning he shows no recollection of the event.

The couple makes a brief stop at the dairy on their way to Marlott. They behave awkwardly together in public. Angel leaves Tess near her village, telling her that he will try to accept her past, but that she should not try to come to him until he comes for her.

SUMMARY: CHAPTER XXXVIII

Tess returns home dolefully and confesses to her mother what has happened. Mrs. Durbeyfield calls her a fool, and Mr. Durbeyfield finds it hard to believe Tess is even married. Tess is miserable at home, and when a letter arrives from Angel informing Tess that he has begun looking for a farm in the north, Tess seizes the excuse to leave and tells her family that she is going to join her husband.

She gives them half of the fifty pounds Angel gave her and leaves her home.

Summary: Chapter XXXIX

Three weeks after their marriage, Angel visits his parents and tells them he is traveling to Brazil and not taking Tess. His parents are alarmed and disappointed, but Angel tells them they will meet Tess in a year, when he returns.

Angel's parents surprise him by reading a biblical passage about how virtuous wives are loving, loyal, selfless, and "working." Mrs. Clare applies the passage directly to Tess, demonstrating her whole-hearted acceptance of Angel's choice not to marry a fine lady, but Angel, overcome with emotion, leaves the room. Following him, Mrs. Clare guesses that Angel discovered something dishonorable in Tess's past, but he vehemently denies it.

Analysis: Chapters XXXV–XXXIX

Atmosphere is a very important component in these chapters, and as Tess nears the culmination of her tragedy, the sense of mystical gloom intensifies. The old, abandoned, Gothic d'Urberville mansion is a perfect setting for the emotional change that takes place. The setting also mirrors Tess's feelings of emptiness and coldness toward her family legacy. In exploiting the setting for dramatic and psychological effect, Hardy draws heavily on the conventions of Gothic literature, sometimes creating very unrealistic effects.

In a similar vein, the scene in which Angel sleepwalks is Gothic almost to the point of being ridiculous. The scene represents the fact that, while Tess herself is still very much alive, Angel's vision of her is dead. The woman he married does not seem to be the same woman now, and he cannot reconcile the difference. As Alec sexually violated Tess, Tess's past has spiritually violated Angel. It seems inevitable that Angel's idealized, pure vision of Tess must shatter and, given the importance he attaches to this vision, their marriage must shatter along with it. Angel's reaction is a result of his childish decision to marry the Tess that he envisioned as opposed to Tess as she actually is.

The scene becomes even harder to believe when Angel scoops up his wife, and—still asleep—carries her to her ancestral cemetery and places her in a coffin. Hardy may have included such a scene to please a Victorian readership that loved Gothic gloom and mystery.

But the scene also attests to the hostility of fate toward Tess. Hardy means for us to accept Tess's tragedy as foreordained, willed by the universe, and executed by powers beyond mortal control. By suggesting such a deterministic view of events, Hardy makes us look at the story in a new and unsettling way. For much of the novel, Hardy seems to criticize the archaic and outmoded morality that unfairly judges and condemns Tess, as well as the social hierarchies that allow aristocrats to exploit the lower classes and men to abuse women. But if Tess's tragedy is foreordained, it may not be solely the fault of outdated public moral judgment.

Angel thinks that Tess is somehow dead, and Tess herself actually wants to be dead. She loses her strength and tells Angel that she wishes to submit: "I will obey you, like your wretched slave, even if it is to lie down and die." She never complains about his feelings, and she only criticizes and blames herself. As Angel carries her over the narrow bridge, she imagines both of them falling over the side to their deaths in each other's arms. She wants to commit suicide but—as with her inability to tell Angel about her past—she cannot summon the courage. As they say good-bye, Tess is little more than a walking corpse. Indeed, it seems that Angel has killed her soul and her desire to live. It is apparent now that Tess can never escape the wrongs of the past, either socially or personally.

CHAPTERS XL–XLIV

SUMMARY: CHAPTER XL

Angel puts the jewelry in the bank and arranges to have some additional money sent to Tess, then travels to the Wellbridge Farm to finish some business there. He encounters Izz and impetuously invites her to go to Brazil with him. Izz agrees, and says that she loves him. He asks if she loves him more than Tess, and Izz replies that no one could love him as much as Tess did. Angel sadly takes Izz to her home and leaves for Brazil alone a few days later.

SUMMARY: CHAPTER XLI

Tess finds sporadic work at different dairies and manages to conceal from her family that she is separated from her husband. When her money begins to run low, she is forced to dip into the money Angel left for her. Her parents write to her asking for money to help repair the cottage roof, and she sends them nearly everything she has. In the meantime, Angel is ill and struggling in Brazil as part of a desperate and failing community of British farmers. Even though she is short on money, Tess is too ashamed to ask the Clares for money.

Tess has heard from Marian of a farm where she might find work, and although it is purportedly a difficult place in which to get by, Tess decides to travel there. She encounters the man from Alec d'Urberville's village who accused her of promiscuity in front of Angel and is forced to run and hide from him. She feels as if Alec is hunting her.

Continuing on her way, Tess stumbles upon a flock of pheasants, some of which have died and others that are in agony and pain. She suspects that hunters have shot them and will return to collect them. She feels an affinity for the birds in pain, and she instinctively breaks their necks to kill them and put them out of their misery. Afterward she compares her own plight with that of the pheasants and becomes angry at herself for thinking that she is the most miserable being on Earth.

> *"Poor darlings—to suppose myself the most miserable*
> *being on earth in the sight o' such misery as yours!"*
> *she exclaimed, her tears running down as she killed*
> *the birds tenderly.*   (See QUOTATIONS, p. 57)

SUMMARY: CHAPTER XLII
Tess takes to making herself ugly to protect herself from lustful men, and she cuts off her eyebrows and dresses in old, unattractive clothing. When Tess reaches the farm near the village of Flintcomb-Ash, Marian is curious about Angel, but Tess asks her not to inquire about him. The proprietress of the farm agrees to give Tess a job, and Tess sends her new address to her parents—though she does not acknowledge her marital or financial difficulties.

SUMMARY: CHAPTER XLIII
Tess and Marian work digging up rutabagas in rocky ground. After a time, Izz Huett joins them. They are sent to work in the barn in the winter, and Tess meets the man who owns the farm—it is the same man from Alec d'Urberville's village. He accuses her of being a poor worker, and she offers to work harder to compensate. Marian tells Tess that Angel invited Izz to travel with him to Brazil, and Tess at first feels as though she should write to him. Before long, however, she is overcome by doubt as to whether she really should.

SUMMARY: CHAPTER XLIV

Tess decides to visit Angel's family to discover what has happened to him and begins the long walk to the vicarage. She takes off her boots and hides them, planning to put them on again for the walk home. She overhears Angel's brothers discussing Angel's unfortunate marriage, and when they find her boots, they assume they belong to a peasant. Tess is ashamed and unhappy and decides not to meet Angel's family after all. She begins the walk home, but she stops before a barn in which a passionate sermon is being delivered. She looks inside, and sees none other than Alec d'Urberville.

ANALYSIS: CHAPTERS XL–XLIV

Phase the Fifth, "The Woman Pays," moves the tragic forces of the novel into high gear. When Angel leaves Tess, Tess is too proud to ask his family for help. But since she is also too dutiful toward her own family not to give them half the money he leaves her, her life begins to unravel completely. In other words, because she remains loyal to her sense of self *and* to other people, the situation in which Alec and Angel have placed her becomes impossible. The happiness she knows at Talbothays is completely shattered, and the contrast between jovial Talbothays and cold, hard Flintcomb-Ash hammers home Tess's new life situation.

In these chapters, Angel visits or runs into several family members and acquaintances who all try to tell him that Tess is a noble and loyal wife. When Angel visits his parents, it seems that Angel is more conventional than his parents in his definition of wifely virtue. The Bible passage that they read says nothing about premarital celibacy, but Angel seems to believe that chastity is an absolute virtue. While the Bible passage seems to describe Tess accurately, Angel cannot recognize her in it. He is blinded by his failure to accept Tess for who she really is. In this section, Angel proves himself more judgmental and inflexible than his mother, who turns out to be surprisingly adaptable. When Angel runs into Izz, she freely admits that no one could love him more than Tess, even though she too loves him. But Angel is unable to register these testaments to Tess's worth, as he is still sleepwalking through life. He takes Tess's transgression as a personal attack on him, which makes him unable to see her clearly. Even his family, who has been preoccupied with social distinctions, can actually accept Tess as she is—and they have not even met her.

In addition, the decline of Tess's physical appearance al
cates the sharp downturn in her life: she even cuts off her ey
to make herself unattractive to lustful young men. Tess's ree
ter with Alec d'Urberville is staged at the moment of her greatest
weakness, as she has gone to ask for help from Angel's parents.
While "[grieving] for the beloved man whose unyielding judgment
has caused her all these later sorrows," she encounters the man who
condemned her to that judgment, and the stage is set for Tess's hardest challenge: to avoid the temptation to give in to Alec d'Urberville
again in order to help herself and her family. Hardy has arranged his
story so that Tess's most admirable strengths, such as her loyalty to
her family, tempt her toward her worst mistake. Fate manifests itself
again in Tess's visit to Angel's family, in which her tragic course is
once again influenced by improbable circumstance. Had Tess not
happened to overhear Felix and Cuthbert criticizing Angel's marriage, she might not leave when she does and see Alec at such a
despairing and vulnerable moment. Fate impinges upon Tess's life at
every turn. Often, when faced with a difficult decision, the choice
she selects makes her situation much worse. But her bad decision-
making is not due to a lack of thought and consideration, since Tess
spends entire chapters deliberating about which course to take.
Instead, the consequences of her actions seem predestined. Even in
her spontaneous choices, like her impromptu decision to leave the
church, there is no way Tess could possibly know that she would
then, in turn, run into Alec. Moreover, Alec's conversion from sexual predator to religious preacher appears the most improbable
event of all. For this circumstance, Angel's own father Reverend
Clare is responsible, adding the final surprising touch.

PHASE THE SIXTH:
THE CONVERT, CHAPTERS XLV–XLVIII

SUMMARY: CHAPTER XLV

Tess has not seen Alec since she left his family's service. When she
sees and hears him testifying to his religious conversion, she is
struck dumb with a sudden terror. She withdraws, but Alec sees her
and runs after her, claiming he has to save her soul. He says he has
found God through the intercession of the Reverend Clare. Tess,
angry and disbelieving, excoriates people like Alec, who ruin other
people's lives and then try to secure a place in heaven by suddenly

converting. She then asserts that she cannot put her faith in Alec's religion when a better man than he—meaning Angel—does not believe in that religion. Alec expresses fear of Tess, and as they come to a stone monument called the Cross-in-Hand, he asks Tess to swear that she will never tempt him again. She agrees and Alec leaves, reading a letter from Reverend Clare to calm himself. Tess asks a shepherd what the Cross-in-Hand signifies, and she learns that it is an object of ill omen.

SUMMARY: CHAPTER XLVI

The omen proves correct a few days later, when Alec approaches Tess in the fields and asks her to marry him. He proposes that they go to Africa to be missionaries. Tess replies that she is already married, and she asks the distraught Alec to leave. She begins another letter to Angel but is unable to finish it.

At Candlemas, Alec again approaches Tess. This time, he asks her to pray for him. Tess replies that she cannot pray, and she recites Angel's reasons for doubting the validity of church doctrine. Alec appears shaken, and Tess asserts that she has a religion but no belief in the supernatural. Alec says that he has missed an opportunity to preach in order to see her, and he says that he is bothered by the fact that he has no right to help or protect her, while the man who does have that right has chosen to abandon her. Tess asks him to leave before their conversation can taint her husband's honor.

SUMMARY: CHAPTER XLVII

In early spring, Tess has been assigned a stint of difficult work as a thresher on the farm. Alec appears again, saying that he is no longer a preacher and beseeching Tess to come away with him. He says his love for her has strengthened, and he is upset that her husband neglects her. Tess slaps his face with a leather glove. He becomes angry, but calms himself, asserting his desire to be her master and telling her that he is her true husband. He says he will be back in the afternoon to collect her.

SUMMARY: CHAPTER XLVIII

Alec comes back that afternoon as he promised. He walks Tess home and asks her to trust him to take care of both Tess and her family. Tess again refuses his offers, and that night she writes a letter to Angel, finally confessing her loyalty and her love and asking for his help against the temptation presented by Alec.

ANALYSIS: CHAPTERS XLV–XLVIII

Though Alec d'Urberville seems at first to have undergone a remarkable transformation from a rake into a pious and religious man, he discards this posture so effortlessly and quickly that it seems to have been a superfluous charade—Alec's attempts to contain his desire for Tess seem weak at best. Indeed, we may wonder why Hardy chooses to reintroduce Alec as a convert at this point in the novel, given that he seems to be very much the same man as before. One effect of this choice is to heighten dramatically the bitter irony of Tess's predicament. Tess continues to suffer as a social outcast because of a disgrace that is much more Alec's fault than hers, yet the hypocritical Alec has the luxury to repent and even win acceptance as a preacher. Tess's plight as a woman thus appears incredibly unjust, reinforcing the message given in the subtitle of this section of the novel: "The Woman Pays."

Alec's reintroduction into the novel comes at Tess's lowest moment, but his new pitch still does not work on her. She has not seen Alec for a long time, but she has clearly thought about him and what he did to her. Tess is observant and distrusting of Alec, and she views his conversion as a plot to win her back. The converted Alec appears to her as a wolf in sheep's clothing, intending to prey on her, or like a devil in disguise, come to tempt her a final time. Indeed, we might well view the relationship between Tess and Alec as an allegory of good struggling with the temptation offered by evil.

Alec continues to tempt Tess with money and security, the two things that would help her family the most, and in doing so he tests her ability to resist evil. His promise of financial security is attractive, but not quite attractive enough. Tess has learned her lesson about risking herself and her happiness for the sake of money. She is a much stronger woman now and is more knowledgeable about conniving men, especially Alec. This strength deters Alec and makes him feel weaker and more vulnerable because his plot is not working. Alec is successful, however, in making Tess doubt herself.

As Tess struggles with Alec's temptation, her need for Angel becomes more and more desperate. If Angel were to return to her and do his duty as her husband, her problems would greatly diminish. She writes to Angel and pleads that he not judge her on her irretrievable past. Ironically, Alec asks Tess to do the same thing for him, claiming that he has changed, that Tess tempted him, and that he must not be judged based on his past mistakes. Tess's situation thus makes her very vulnerable to Alec's persuasions. She is obviously heartbroken and needs to be loved more than ever. She is also distraught by her family's ever-worsening financial situation. Alec's reasoning seems more valid to Tess than it has in the past. In a way, Tess and Alec are similar in that they have both fallen and ask for forgiveness for their indiscretions.

CHAPTERS XLIX–LII

SUMMARY: CHAPTER XLIX

Tess's letter goes to Angel's parents, who forward it to Angel in Brazil. Mrs. Clare reproaches her husband for keeping Angel from attending Cambridge, whereas Reverend Clare feels justified in his decision but regrets the misery his son has endured. For his part, Angel is ready to abandon his idea of farming in Brazil. The suffering he has endured there has softened his feelings toward Tess, and when a more experienced man tells him he was wrong to leave her, Angel feels a powerful regret. When the man dies a few days later, his words assume even more power in Angel's mind. Back at the farm, Tess encounters her sister, Liza-Lu, who comes with sorrowful news: Tess's mother is dying, and her father is also very ill and can do no work. Tess tells Izz and Marian what has happened and leaves for home the next morning.

SUMMARY: CHAPTER L

Upon her arrival, Tess does what she can to make her mother comfortable and then begins working in the garden and on the family's land. One night, she looks over and sees Alec working next to her. He again offers to help Tess and her family. She is sorely tempted but declines again. Enraged, Alec leaves.

On the way home, Tess's sister tells her that their father has died, which means that Tess's family will lose their house. John Durbeyfield was the last person guaranteed a place in the terms of the lease, and the tenant farmer who owns the house wants to use it for his own workers.

SUMMARY: CHAPTER LI

Tess prepares to move her family to a set of rooms in Kingsbere. Alec arrives and tells Tess the legend of the ghostly d'Urberville Coach—the message of which is that the sound of an invisible coach is a bad omen. Alec tries to persuade Tess to move her family to his family's garden home, allow him to send her brothers and sisters to school, and have Tess's mother tend the fowls. Tess is again sorely tempted, but she once more declines Alec's offer, and he rides away. As he leaves, Tess admits to herself that Angel has treated her badly, and she writes him a letter saying she will do all she can to forget him, since she will never be able to forgive him. Joan asks what Alec said to her, but Tess refuses to divulge the story, saying she will tell her mother when they are in their rooms at Kingsbere.

SUMMARY: CHAPTER LII

> "The little finger of the sham d'Urberville can do more for you than the whole dynasty of the real underneath. . . . Now command me. What shall I do?" (See QUOTATIONS, p. 58)

The next day, Tess and her family begin their journey. On the way, they meet Marian and Izz, who are moving on to new work at a new farm. When they reach Kingsbere, they learn that Joan's letter was late, and the rooms have already been rented. They cannot find more lodging and end up sleeping in the churchyard, in a plot called d'Urberville Aisle. Tess finds Alec lying on a tomb, and he tells her he can do more for her than all her noble ancestors. Tess tells him to leave, and angrily he does, promising that Tess will learn to be civil. Tess leans down toward the funeral vault and asks why she is still alive. Marian and Izz do their part for their friend by writing a note to Angel asking him to go back to Tess.

ANALYSIS

Phase the Sixth tells the story of Tess's struggle to remain free from Alec despite her family's increasingly desperate plight, which Alec has the power to alleviate if Tess agrees to love him. Though Alec overtly plays the part of a villain in this section, the real conflict is within Tess, as two of her deepest virtues, her integrity and her loyalty to her family, prompt her in opposite directions. Her integrity demands that she stay away from Alec, whom she does not love, but her duty to her family tempts her to go with him to save her mother and her siblings. Integrity wins out throughout the section, but we get the sense that it is only a matter of time before Tess is forced to submit. As a result, the story in this section and part of the next is propelled along by a kind of race: Angel needs to forgive Tess and return to her before she surrenders to Alec.

In fact, Angel is in the process of changing as a result of his bad experiences in Brazil. He begins to alter his attitude toward Tess, slowly realizing that his way of thinking has been faulty. He undergoes an emotional and moral conversion that is much more real than Alec's religious conversion a few chapters back. Angel is finally shedding his immaturity and growing to love Tess as a responsible adult. But the distance between Angel and Tess is still great, both physically and emotionally. Ironically, the distance may have led them closer together, as their loneliness and separation have shown Angel how much Tess means to him. Notably, Angel's transformation comes when he is at a great distance from English society and its prevailing sentiments. Even though he remains the die-hard progressive of the Clares, the pressure of conforming to English propriety coupled with his troubled view of his marriage stifles Angel's growth while in England.

As Alec's courtship of Tess increases in intensity, so too does the string of misfortunes that plague Tess and her family. With her options narrowing, Tess becomes more desperate in her desire to reconcile with Angel: "Come to me!" she pleads, "Come to me and save me from what threatens me!" Throughout, Alec is portrayed as a sinister and threatening figure even when supposedly in the grip of religious conflict—at one point, the narrator notes that his face blackens "with something that was not Christianity." Even when he appears most in love with Tess, he still seems the same old Alec, thinly disguised, hoping to seduce Tess by doing a good turn for her.

The supernatural, Gothic atmosphere of the old d'Urberville mansion reappears here at the d'Urberville Aisle in the churchyard. Here, Tess, a real d'Urberville, and Alec, an imposter, have one of their most solemn moments, as Alec asserts that he can do more for Tess than all her lofty dead ancestors. Tess begins to realize the futility of claiming such an aristocratic legacy, since her ancestors truly cannot help her at all. She begins to realize that Alec may be her only hope. In the yard, Alec's legend of the d'Urberville Coach evokes the Gothic or supernatural yet again, providing an ill omen that foreshadows the deadly conclusion of their story.

PHASE THE SEVENTH: THE FULFILLMENT, CHAPTERS LIII–LIX

SUMMARY: CHAPTER LIII

Angel returns to his parents' home, haggard and gaunt after his tribulations abroad. He reads Tess's angry letter, and he worries that she will never forgive him. His mother haughtily declares that he should not worry about the opinions of a poor commoner, and Angel reveals to her Tess's exalted lineage.

Angel spends a few days at home regaining his strength. He writes a letter to Tess addressed to Marlott, and finally receives a reply from Tess's mother informing him that they have left Marlott and that Tess is no longer with the family.

After a short time spent waiting, Angel decides that he must not delay his reunion with Tess. He is encouraged in this feeling by the revelation that Tess has not used any of the money Angel left with his father. Angel realizes that Tess must have suffered great poverty while he was abroad, and he is overcome with pity and guilt. Angel's parents finally guess the secret cause of their son's estrangement from Tess, and find that the knowledge disposes them to feel more kindly toward their daughter-in-law. Just before Angel leaves, he receives the letter from Marian and Izz.

SUMMARY: CHAPTER LIV

Angel sets out to find his wife, traveling through the farm at Flintcomb-Ash and through Marlott, where he learns of the death of Tess's father. He finds the elaborate gravestone of John Durbeyfield, and when he learns that it is unpaid for, he settles the bill. When he meets Joan, he finds his mother-in-law uncomfortable and hesitant to tell him where Tess has gone. At last she takes pity on him and reveals that Tess is in Sandbourne.

SUMMARY: CHAPTER LV

In Sandbourne, Angel is unable to find a Mrs. Clare or a Miss Durbeyfield, but he does learn that a d'Urberville is staying at an expensive lodging called The Herons.

Angel hurries to The Herons and is impressed by its grandeur. He wonders how Tess could possibly afford it and thinks she must have sold his godmother's diamonds. When Tess appears, she is dressed in expensive clothing. Angel pleads for her forgiveness and tells her that he has learned to accept her as she is and desperately wants her to come back to him. Brokenhearted, Tess replies that it is too late—thinking Angel would never come back for her, she gave in to Alec d'Urberville's desires and is now under his protection. Tess leaves the room, and Angel rushes out of the house.

Summary: Chapter LVI

Mrs. Brooks, the landlady at The Herons, follows Tess upstairs and spies on her through the keyhole. She sees Tess holding her head in her hands, accusing Alec of deceiving her into thinking that Angel would never come back for her. Alec replies angrily, and Mrs. Brooks, startled, flees the scene. Back in her own room, she sees Tess go through the front gate, where she disappears onto the street. A short while later, Mrs. Brooks notices a dark red spot spreading on the ceiling. Terrified, Mrs. Brooks has a workman open the door of the d'Urberville rooms, where they discover Alec lying on the bed, stabbed to death. The landlady gives the alarm, and the news of Alec's murder quickly spreads through the town.

Summary: Chapter LVII

Angel decides to leave on the first train. At his hotel, he finds a telegraph from his mother informing him that Cuthbert is going to marry Mercy Chant. Rather than waiting for the train, Angel decides to walk to the next station and meet it there. As he hikes out of the valley, he sees Tess running after him. He draws her off the main road, and she tells him that she has killed Alec. Tess says she had to kill Alec because he wronged Angel, but that she also had to return to Alec because Angel abandoned her. She begs Angel's forgiveness, and he, thinking she is delirious, tells her he loves her. At last he realizes she is serious, though he still does not believe she has actually killed Alec. He agrees to protect her.

They walk toward the interior of the country, waiting for the search for Tess to be called off so they can escape overseas. That evening, they find an old mansion and slip in through the windows. After a woman comes to close up the house, Angel opens the shutters, and they are alone for the night.

Summary: Chapter LVIII

Five days pass, and Angel and Tess slowly lapse back into their original love. They make little mention of their estrangement. One day the woman who airs the house discovers their hiding place, and they decide it is time to leave. After a day of travel, they arrive in the evening at Stonehenge, where Tess feels quite at home. As she rests by a pillar, she says that she feels as if there are no people in the world but them.

Tess becomes distraught, and asks Angel to look after Liza-Lu when Tess is dead. She says she hopes Angel will marry Liza-Lu, then asks her husband if he believes they will meet again after death. Angel does not answer, and Tess, upset, drifts into sleep.

At dawn, Angel realizes that they are surrounded. Men are moving in from all sides, and Angel realizes Tess must truly have killed Alec. Angel asks the men not to take Tess until she wakes. When she sees them, she feels strangely relieved. Tess is glad she will not live, because she feels unworthy of Angel's love.

SUMMARY: CHAPTER LIX

> *"Justice" was done, and the President of the Immortals (in Aeschylean phrase) had ended his sport with Tess.*   (See QUOTATIONS, p. 59)

Sometime later, from a hillside outside Wintoncester, Angel and Liza-Lu watch as a black flag is raised above the tower. Tess has been put to death. Angel and Liza-Lu are motionless for a time, and then they join hands and go on.

_____

ANALYSIS: CHAPTERS LIII–LIX

Phase the Seventh brings the novel to a tragic close through a shift in perspective. It begins in an aura of mystery, as Hardy chooses not to narrate the climax of Tess's struggle—her return to the bed of Alec d'Urberville. The first part of this section is told instead from Angel's perspective. When he arrives at The Herons, we have a gradual, sickening sense of what to expect, but Angel has no idea. He is too late because the race is over, and Tess's loyalty to her family has overmastered her integrity. Torn apart, Tess now kills her lover in a murderous rage out of love for her husband. From that moment, the novel simply becomes a mechanical process leading to the inevitable conclusion—Tess's death.

As Angel returns with renewed loyalty and love for Tess, it becomes apparent that Alec has considerably broken down Tess's loyalty to Angel. Tess recovers this love and loyalty when she sees Angel again, and she feels guilty about how far she has drifted. Her pride in poverty when Angel is away stands in direct contrast with her fancy clothing and luxurious lodging, which physically measures how far into temptation she has gone with Alec. Her shame and grief cause her violent side to explode, and she kills Alec. Whether intentionally or not, Tess has fulfilled Angel's proclamation that they cannot be together as long as Alec is alive. The murder may appear justified to us at this point, after everything through which Alec has put Tess. But, though we may sympathize with Tess's actions, we know that Tess must now flee and live the life of a hunted criminal.

The short section narrated from the perspective of Mrs. Brooks is almost an exact double of the technique Hardy uses with Angel at the beginning of Phase the Seventh. Just as he excludes Tess's return to Alec, he excludes her murder of Alec. Just as an unsuspecting third party shows us that she has gone back to him, another unsuspecting third party shows us that she has killed him. Tess's mind has been at the center of the novel from its beginning, and practically everything that has happened has been shown solely in its relation to her. By shifting attention away from her so suddenly, Hardy creates the sense that Tess is already lost—though she is still alive, she has partially vanished into the gloom of her fate. At the end, despite the atmosphere of Gothic mystery and supernatural portent that infuses much of the novel, Hardy still manages to surprise us by setting the conclusion at Stonehenge, one of the most famous and mysterious monuments in the world.

Important Quotations Explained

1. "Don't you really know, Durbeyfield, that you are the lineal representative of the ancient and knightly family of the d'Urbervilles, who derive their descent from Sir Pagan d'Urberville, that renowned knight who came from Normandy with William the Conqueror, as appears by Battle Abbey Roll?" "Never heard it before, sir!"

In this passage, from Chapter I, the local parson informs Mr. Durbeyfield of his grand lineage, thus setting in motion the events that change the fate of Tess Durbeyfield forever. Interestingly, the parson's tone is casual, as if he is unable even to conceive of how his news might lead to tragedy later. For the parson it is genealogical trivia, but for Durbeyfield it feels like fate—the deepest truth about himself, like Oedipus's discovery of his own identity. The fact that this prophetic news is delivered on the road, in an open field, right at the beginning of the work is reminiscent of the opening of *Macbeth*. There, the witches address Macbeth as "Thane of Cawdor" and "King of Scotland," just as the parson addresses Durbeyfield as "Sir John." As in Macbeth's case, the noble address leads to disaster and death—in this case, the death of the "rightful" d'Urberville, Alec.

Hardy emphasizes the irony of Durbeyfield's situation not only by contrasting the common peddler on the road with the image of the "renowned knight" who was his forebear, but also by contrasting the modes of address of Durbeyfield and the parson. The parson has just addressed him as "Sir John," which sets the whole conversation in motion, but we see here that the parson soon lapses back into the familiar tone more appropriate to one addressing a social inferior: "Don't you really know, Durbeyfield. . . . " Durbeyfield does the same: despite his discovery that he is Sir John, it is he who calls the parson "sir" here. The ironies multiply, making questions of class and identity complex and unstable, as Hardy intends to depict them.

2.   Clare came close, and bent over her. "Dead, dead, dead!" he murmured. After fixedly regarding her for some moments with the same gaze of unmeasurable woe he bent lower, enclosed her in his arms, and rolled her in the sheet as in a shroud. Then lifting her from the bed with as much respect as one would show to a dead body, he carried her across the room, murmuring, "My poor poor Tess, my dearest darling Tess! So sweet, so good, so true!" The words of endearment, withheld so severely in his waking hours, were inexpressibly sweet to her forlorn and hungry heart. If it had been to save her weary life she would not, by moving or struggling, have put an end to the position she found herself in. Thus she lay in absolute stillness, scarcely venturing to breathe, and, wondering what he was going to do with her, suffered herself to be borne out upon the landing. "My wife— dead, dead!" he said.

QUOTATIONS

In Chapter XXXVII, Angel Clare begins to sleepwalk on the third night of his estrangement from Tess, having rejected her as his wife because of her earlier disgrace. Like Lady Macbeth's sleepwalking scene, Angel's nighttime somnambulism reveals an inner conflict within a character who earlier seems convinced of a moral idea, in control, and inflexible. For Lady Macbeth, her earlier cold protestations that killing a king is justifiable are belied by her unconscious fixation on being bloodstained. For Angel, the situation is reversed. He consciously maintains a conviction that Tess is bad, corrupt, and cannot be forgiven, but his unconscious sleepwalking self reveals the tender love and moral respect for her ("so good, so true!") that he feels somewhere inside him. This revelation foreshadows his final realization, too late, that his condemnation of Tess was wrong-headed. Angel's words "dead, dead, dead" hint at Tess's future death, but they also signal Angel's conception of Tess. She is alive physically, but for him she is dead morally, as dead as an idea of purity that he once revered.

3.   Under the trees several pheasants lay about, their rich
plumage dabbled with blood; some were dead, some
feebly twitching a wing, some staring up at the sky,
some pulsating quickly, some contorted, some
stretched out—all of them writhing in agony except
the fortunate ones whose tortures had ended during
the night by the inability of nature to bear more. With
the impulse of a soul who could feel for kindred
sufferers as much as for herself, Tess's first thought
was to put the still living birds out of their torture,
and to this end with her own hands she broke the
necks of as many as she could find, leaving them to lie
where she had found them till the gamekeepers should
come, as they probably would come, to look for them
a second time. "Poor darlings—to suppose myself the
most miserable being on earth in the sight o' such
misery as yours!" she exclaimed, her tears running
down as she killed the birds tenderly.

Tess stumbles upon the pheasants at the end of Chapter XLI, feeling
like a "hunted soul." The dying birds symbolize her own condition.
It is a strange and unexpected image, since throughout all the scenes
of farm life we have witnessed in the novel, there has never been any
killing. Farming is always associated with production, never with
loss or sacrifice. But hunting is different: it kills creatures, and does
so unnecessarily. It is gratuitous cruelty. The image of silently suffering victims of violence evokes Tess's quiet acceptance of her own
violation at the hands of Alec, which was also gratuitous. In a literary sense, these flightless birds stand in sharp contrast to the high-
flying birds of Romantic poetry—we recall that Angel is compared
to Shelley, who wrote an ode to a skylark. Romantic birds leave the
Earth below to soar into a higher plane of existence, but the birds
here have no such luck, having been shot down as Tess has been.

   Tess's killing of these suffering birds suggests that she is killing off
that part of herself that has quietly accepted many years of agony.
After this scene Tess begins to show a more active resolution that
culminates in her final murder of Alec. Her newfound activity may
not save her; indeed, her punishment for the murder, presumably
death by hanging, will snap her neck just like she snaps the necks of
these pheasants. Nevertheless, it may be preferable to her earlier
passivity, providing her with a nobler way to face her fate.

4.   As soon as she drew close to it she discovered all in a
        moment that the figure was a living person; and the
        shock to her sense of not having been alone was so
        violent that she was quite overcome, and sank down
        nigh to fainting, not however till she had recognized
        Alec d'Urberville in the form. He leapt off the slab and
        supported her. "I saw you come in," he said smiling,
        "and got up there not to interrupt your meditations. A
        family gathering, is it not, with these old fellows under
        us here? Listen." He stamped with his heel heavily on
        the floor; whereupon there arose a hollow echo from
        below. "That shook them a bit, I'll warrant," he
        continued. "And you thought I was the mere stone
        reproduction of one of them. But no. The old order
        changeth. The little finger of the sham d'Urberville can
        do more for you than the whole dynasty of the real
        underneath. . . . Now command me. What shall I do?"

Having sought shelter for her family in the ancient clan's church in Chapter LII, Tess has gone out walking at night and has come upon her family vault and Alec d'Urberville. Hardy's irony is deep here: originally, the knowledge that Tess belongs to the d'Urberville line brings her into tragic conflict with Alec, and here those ancestors and Alec are united before her dazed eyes. The two main factors in her sad fate are brought together for her viewing. Moreover, it is ironic that Alec is at first mistaken for one of the sculpted ancestors, as if the distinction between the truly noble d'Urbervilles and the "sham" ones—to use Alec's own word—is not as important as it first seemed. They are all part of the same display. Whether true or fake, the d'Urbervilles have brought Tess only grief. When Alec stomps on the floor of the crypt and a "hollow echo from below" is heard, we feel that those ancestors may indeed be nothing more than an empty void, a meaningless nothingness. Alec believes he is different from them, since he has power over her while they do not, but in fact he is just like them, using his power like a grand lord although he is quite hollow. He promises empty advantages to her, like the wealth she eventually receives from him, that can never be more important than love. This scene in the corpse-ridden vault shows how *dead* all thoughts of personal grandeur are next to the life of true feeling, like that of Tess's feelings for Angel.

5.   "Justice" was done, and the President of the
Immortals (in Aeschylean phrase) had ended his sport
with Tess. And the d'Urberville knights and dames
slept on in their tombs unknowing. The two
speechless gazers bent themselves down to the earth,
as if in prayer, and remained there a long time,
absolutely motionless: the flag continued to wave
silently. As soon as they had strength they arose,
joined hands again, and went on.

This passage is the last paragraph of Chapter LIX at the close of *Tess of the d'Urbervilles*. Its tired and unimpassioned tone suggests the narrator's weariness with the ways of the world, as if quite familiar with the fact that life always unfolds in this way. Nothing great is achieved by this finale: the two figures of Liza-Lu and Angel "went on" at the end, just as life itself will go on. Ignorance rules, rather than understanding: the d'Urberville ancestors who cause the tragedy are not even moved from their slumber, blithely unaffected by the agony and death of one of their own line. Tess's tale has not been a climactic unfolding, but a rather humdrum affair that perhaps happens all the time.

In this sense, there is great irony in Hardy's reference to the Greek tragedian Aeschylus, since we feel tragedy should be more impassioned, like the *Prometheus Bound* referred to here. Prometheus dared to steal fire from the gods for the benefit of men, thus improving human life, but he was punished by eternal agony sent by the president of the gods. Aeschylus's view of that divine justice was ironic—just as Hardy's justice is placed in ironic quotation marks—since it seemed deeply unjust to punish Prometheus so severely. Our judgment of Prometheus's crime matters immensely. Yet Tess's suffering, by contrast, seems simply a game or "sport," as if nothing important is at stake. It is hard to know whether Tess has brought any benefits to anyone, though Angel's life has been changed and Liza-Lu may grow up to be like her sister. In any case, Hardy hints that Tess's life may have a mythical and tragic importance like that of Prometheus, but it is up to us to judge how ironic this justice is, or what her life's importance might be.

KEY FACTS

FULL TITLE
Tess of the d'Urbervilles

AUTHOR
Thomas Hardy

TYPE OF WORK
Novel

GENRE
Victorian, tragic

LANGUAGE
English

TIME AND PLACE WRITTEN
1880s, England

DATE OF FIRST PUBLICATION
1891

PUBLISHER
Random House, but also published serially in different periodicals

NARRATOR
Anonymous

POINT OF VIEW
The narrator speaks in the third person, and looks deep into the characters' minds. The narrator is objective but has an omniscient understanding of future implications of characters' actions as they happen.

TONE
Realistic, pessimistic

TENSE
Past

SETTING (TIME)
The 1880s and 1890s

KEY FACTS

SETTING (PLACE)
Wessex, the southwest of England

PROTAGONIST
Tess Durbeyfield

MAJOR CONFLICT
Tess is seduced, impregnated, and abandoned by the son of her upper-class patroness, making her unacceptable to her true love Angel later in life.

RISING ACTION
Tess's family's discovery that they are ancient English aristocracy, giving them all fantasies of a higher station in life; Tess's accidental killing of the family horse, which drives her to seek help from the d'Urbervilles, where she is seduced and dishonored.

CLIMAX
Tess's new husband discovers her earlier seduction by Alec and decides to leave her, going off to Brazil and not answering her letters, and bringing Tess to despair.

FALLING ACTION
Tess's last-ditch decision to marry Alec, who claims to love her; Angel's return from Brazil to discover Tess marriage to her former seducer, and his meeting with Tess; Tess's murder of Alec and short-lived escape with Angel before being apprehended and executed

THEMES
The injustice of existence; changing ideas of social class in Victorian England; men dominating women

MOTIFS
Birds; the Book of Genesis; variant names

SYMBOLS
Prince; the d'Urberville family vault; Brazil

FORESHADOWING
Tess's killing of the pheasants foreshadows her own death by hanging; Alec's assertion that he will "master" Tess again foreshadows his reemergence in her life

STUDY QUESTIONS & ESSAY TOPICS

STUDY QUESTIONS

1. *Discuss the character of Tess. To what extent is she a helpless victim? When is she strong and when is she weak?*

Tess is a young woman who tends to find herself in the wrong place at the wrong time. She is a victim, but she is also, at times, irresponsible. She falls asleep while taking the beehives to market, which ends up killing the family horse, Prince. She decides to visit the d'Urbervilles in Trantridge, giving rise to all her future woes, partly out of the guilt and responsibility she feels toward her family. She wants to make good, but in trying to help her family she loses sight of her own safety and her own wants and wishes. She becomes Alec's victim in the forest. She probably should have known not to put herself in such a situation, but she has few other options. Here, it seems as though she is destined to rely on others, even when they are unreliable.

But Tess is also a strong woman throughout the novel. She stands up for herself and refuses to crumble under pressure. She chastises herself for her weakness after her sexual escapade with Alec. If we agree with her claim that this indiscretion is a moment of weakness, we probably also feel that such weakness is not unlike that of most human beings. She is hard on herself for letting herself become a victim. At the burial of her child, Sorrow, she weeps but collects herself and moves on as a stronger woman. Overall, her determined attempts to escape her past primarily reflect her strength.

2. *Discuss the role of landscape in the novel. How do descriptions of place match the development of the story? Does the passing of the seasons play any symbolic role?*

The landscape always seems to inform us about the emotion and character of the event. Whjen the novel opens at the village dance, the sun is out and the day is beautiful. This celebration is where Tess and Angel meet, even if only briefly. The weather turns as Tess returns home, where the scene is less elegant. Throughout the novel, many of the bad events occur in a dark and deep forest, and Alec and Tess interact numerous times in such a forest.

The seasons bring changes to the story as well. At Talbothays Dairy, the summer is full of budding love between Tess and Angel. When they profess their love for each other, it begins to rain, but neither one cares: the weather cannot affect them. When they separate, Angel goes to Brazil and finds the farming extremely difficult, while Tess goes to work at the farm at Flintcomb-Ash, where the work in the rugged, depressing stubble fields is harsh and grueling.

3. *Hardy rarely questions public morality openly in* Tess of the d'Urbervilles. *Nevertheless, the novel has been taken as a powerful critique of the social principles that were dominant in Tess's time. How does Hardy achieve this effect? Why might we infer a level of social criticism beneath Tess's story?*

Our sense that *Tess of the d'Urbervilles* implicitly criticizes Hardy's society owes much to Hardy's use of a classical tragic plot ending in an undeserved punishment. Tess's story contains many features of Greek tragedy, as Hardy's reference at the end of the novel to Aeschylus's *Prometheus Bound* reminds us. The classical tragic hero, according to Aristotle, is noble and dignified, and is punished on a far greater scale than his small sins warrant, with death. Tess too is highborn and honorable, and her momentary submission to Alec brings her a far greater suffering than she deserves, as even Alec comes to realize. In addition, as is usual with the demise of tragic heroes, Tess's execution feels more significant than a mere death—it feels like a great and noble sacrifice to some higher power's will. But in her case, the higher power is not the gods, but Victorian social forces. It is the Victorian cult of aristocratic lineage that drives Tess to seek the patronage of Mrs. d'Urberville and meet her seducer Alec. It is the unfair class system that allows a rich nobleman to impregnate and abandon a lower-class girl without consequences. It is also the Victorian myth of the pure virginal bride that unfairly keeps Angel from accepting Tess as his wife, despite his own besmirched sexual history. These social injustices bring undeserved suffering to Tess, as the ancient gods brought undeserved suffering to the tragic hero. It is thus the tragic structure of *Tess of the d'Urbervilles* that causes us feel indignation at the unfairness of Victorian society, without the need for any outright denunciations by the author.

QUESTIONS & ESSAYS

SUGGESTED ESSAY TOPICS

1. What is the role of fate in *Tess of the d'Urbervilles*? What does Hardy mean by "fate"? To what extent does Tess's tragedy hinge on improbable coincidence?

2. Throughout Tess's story, a number of sources are presented as possible moral authorities and possible guides on which characters might base their moral choices. What are some of these sources? Which of them, if any, prevails?

3. Discuss the character of Alec. Is he the villain of the novel? Does he really love Tess? In what ways does he exemplify the novel's critique of the upper class?

4. Tess's story is full of omens, and her tragedy is largely prefigured by all the bad omens that occur throughout her story. What are some of these omens? Are they an effective device? Do they build suspense, or are they simply a kind of heavy-handed foreshadowing?

5. Social class and lineage are powerful forces for determining character in the novel. What role does Tess's noble lineage play in the depiction of her character? With regard to noble blood, is it possible that the novel's portrayal of Tess advances some of the very social stereotypes it otherwise criticizes?

6. Hardy's style has been praised as rhythmic and imaginative, and also criticized as clunky and rough-edged. How is Hardy's style best characterized? What are some of its other characteristics?

REVIEW & RESOURCES

QUIZ

1. The action of the novel takes place in what area of England?

   A. Essex
   B. Sussex
   C. Wessex
   D. London

2. Which of the following does John Durbeyfield learn at the beginning of the novel?

   A. That he has lost his job
   B. That he comes from an aristocratic family
   C. That he won the lottery
   D. That he is a prince

3. Angel and Tess first see each other at:

   A. The market
   B. The May Day dance
   C. Trantridge
   D. Talbothays Dairy

4. Who tells Angel that Tess has gone to Sandbourne?

   A. Mrs. Brooks
   B. Reverend Clare
   C. Alec
   D. Mrs. Durbeyfield

5. After Angel picks up Tess while sleepwalking, where does he place her?

   A. In a coffin
   B. In their bed
   C. On a rock
   D. On a bridge

6. Which of these women is *not* a milkmaid?

    A. Marian
    B. Izz
    C. Mercy
    D. Retty

7. Angel plays which musical instrument?

    A. The harpsichord
    B. The accordion
    C. The harp
    D. The guitar

8. In what town did Tess grow up?

    A. Kingsbere
    B. Trantridge
    C. Sandbourne
    D. Marlott

9. Why can't Mr. Durbeyfield make the trip to the market?

    A. He is too sick
    B. He is too tired
    C. He is too old
    D. He is too drunk

10. What advice does Mrs. Durbeyfield give Tess?

    A. Not to tell Angel her secret
    B. Not to tell Alec her secret
    C. To leave Alec
    D. To marry Alec

11. How much money does Angel give to Tess?

    A. 100 shillings
    B. 100 pounds
    C. 50 pounds
    D. 50 shillings

12. How much of the money does Tess initially give to her family?

    A. 25 shillings
    B. 25 pounds
    C. 50 pounds
    D. 50 shillings

13. What part of the house do the Durbeyfields need to repair?

    A. The floor
    B. The wall
    C. The roof
    D. The door

14. Where is the Talbothays Dairy located?

    A. The Valley of the Herons
    B. The Valley of Marlott
    C. The Valley of the Great Dairies
    D. The Valley of the Small Dairies

15. Who does Cuthbert Clare marry?

    A. Izz
    B. Mercy Chant
    C. Liza-Lu
    D. Marian

16. Midway through the novel, Alec becomes a:

    A. Farmer
    B. Preacher
    C. Traveling salesman
    D. Nice guy

17. Who is primarily responsible for Prince's death?

    A. Mr. Durbeyfield
    B. Parson Tringham
    C. Abraham
    D. Tess

18. Angel leaves England to farm where?

    A. America
    B. Italy
    C. Brazil
    D. Argentina

19. What is the stone monument called on which Alec makes Tess swear?

    A. Stonehenge
    B. Poor Man's Pass
    C. Cross-in-Hand
    D. The Rosetta Stone

20. Which of these people or animals does Tess *not* kill?

    A. The pheasants
    B. Alec
    C. Sorrow, her baby
    D. Prince, the horse

21. What is the name of the bar to which the Durbeyfield's go?

    A. McSorely's
    B. Rolliver's
    C. Heffernan's
    D. Ye Olde Pubbe

22. What does Tess confess to Angel on their wedding night?

    A. That she lied about her age
    B. That she does not love him
    C. That she is not a virgin
    D. That she ran away from home

23. Liza-Lu is Tess's:

    A. Daughter
    B. Sister
    C. Mother
    D. Friend

24. How does Alec die?

    A. He commits suicide
    B. Angel kills him
    C. Tess kills him
    D. He does not die

25. How does Tess die?

    A. Pneumonia
    B. She is hanged
    C. Angel kills her
    D. Heartache

SUGGESTIONS FOR FURTHER READING

Beer, Gillian. "Descent and Sexual Selection: Women in Narrative." In *Tess of the d'Urbervilles,* ed. by Scott Elledge. New York: W.W. Norton and Company, 1991: 446-451.

Bloom, Harold. *Thomas Hardy's Tess of the d'Urbervilles.* New York: Chelsea House, 1987.

Casagrande, Peter J. *Tess of the d'Urbervilles: Unorthodox Beauty.* New York: Maxwell Macmillan International, 1992.

LAIRD, J. T. *The Shaping of* TESS OF THE D'URBERVILLES. Oxford: Clarendon Press, 1975.

LAVALLEY, ALBERT J. *Twentieth Century Interpretations of* TESS OF THE D'URBE RVILLES. Englewood Cliffs, New Jersey: Prentice-Hall, 1969.

MILLS, SARA, ed. *Feminist Readings/Feminists Reading.* New York: Prentice Hall, 1996.

PARKINSON, MICHAEL H. *The Rural Novel: Jeremias Gotthelf, Thomas Hardy, C.F. Ramuz.* New York: P. Lang, 1984.

Van Ghent, Dorothy. "On *Tess of the d'Urbervilles.*" In *The English Novel: Form and Function.* New York: Holt, Rinehart and Winston, 1964.

WIDDOWSON, PETER, ed. *Tess of the d'Urbervilles: Thomas Hardy.* Hampshire: Macmillan, 1993.

WRIGHT, TERENCE. *Tess of the d'Urbervilles.* Hampshire: Macmillan Publishers, 1987.

SPARKNOTES
TEST PREPARATION
GUIDES

The SparkNotes team figured it was time to cut standardized tests down to size. We've studied the tests for you, so that SparkNotes test prep guides are:

Smarter:
Packed with critical-thinking skills and test-
taking strategies that will improve your score.

Better:
Fully up to date, covering all new features of the tests,
with study tips on every type of question.

Faster:
Our books cover exactly what you need to
know for the test. No more, no less.

SparkNotes Guide to the SAT & PSAT
SparkNotes Guide to the SAT & PSAT — Deluxe Internet Edition
SparkNotes Guide to the ACT
SparkNotes Guide to the ACT — Deluxe Internet Edition
SparkNotes Guide to the SAT II Writing
SparkNotes Guide to the SAT II U.S. History
SparkNotes Guide to the SAT II Math Ic
SparkNotes Guide to the SAT II Math IIc
SparkNotes Guide to the SAT II Biology
SparkNotes Guide to the SAT II Physics

SparkNotes Study Guides:

1984

The Adventures of
    Huckleberry Finn

The Adventures of
    Tom Sawyer

The Aeneid

All Quiet on the
    Western Front

And Then There
    Were None

Angela's Ashes

Animal Farm

Anne of Green Gables

Antony and Cleopatra

As I Lay Dying

As You Like It

The Awakening

The Bean Trees

The Bell Jar

Beloved

Beowulf

Billy Budd

Black Boy

Bless Me, Ultima

The Bluest Eye

Brave New World

The Brothers
    Karamazov

The Call of the Wild

Candide

The Canterbury Tales

Catch-22

The Catcher in the Rye

The Chosen

Cold Mountain

Cold Sassy Tree

The Color Purple

The Count of
    Monte Cristo

Crime and Punishment

The Crucible

Cry, the Beloved
    Country

Cyrano de Bergerac

Death of a Salesman

The Diary of a
    Young Girl

Doctor Faustus

A Doll's House

Don Quixote

Dr. Jekyll and Mr. Hyde

Dracula

Dune

Emma

Ethan Frome

Fahrenheit 451

Fallen Angels

A Farewell to Arms

Flowers for Algernon

The Fountainhead

Frankenstein

The Glass Menagerie

Gone With the Wind

The Good Earth

The Grapes of Wrath

Great Expectations

The Great Gatsby

Gulliver's Travels

Hamlet

The Handmaid's Tale

Hard Times

Harry Potter and the
    Sorcerer's Stone

Heart of Darkness

Henry IV, Part I

Henry V

Hiroshima

The Hobbit

The House of the
    Seven Gables

I Know Why the
    Caged Bird Sings

The Iliad

Inferno

Invisible Man

Jane Eyre

Johnny Tremain

The Joy Luck Club

Julius Caesar

The Jungle

The Killer Angels

King Lear

The Last of the
    Mohicans

Les Misérables

A Lesson Before
    Dying

The Little Prince

Little Women

Lord of the Flies

Macbeth

Madame Bovary

A Man for All Seasons

The Mayor of
    Casterbridge

The Merchant of
    Venice

A Midsummer
    Night's Dream

Moby-Dick

Much Ado About
    Nothing

My Ántonia

Mythology

Native Son

The New Testament

Night

The Odyssey

The Oedipus Trilogy

Of Mice and Men

The Old Man and
    the Sea

The Old Testament

Oliver Twist

The Once and
    Future King

One Flew Over the
    Cuckoo's Nest

One Hundred Years
    of Solitude

Othello

Our Town

The Outsiders

Paradise Lost

The Pearl

The Picture of
    Dorian Gray

A Portrait of the Artist
    as a Young Man

Pride and Prejudice

The Prince

A Raisin in the Sun

The Red Badge of
    Courage

The Republic

Richard III

Robinson Crusoe

Romeo and Juliet

The Scarlet Letter

A Separate Peace

Silas Marner

Sir Gawain and the
    Green Knight

Slaughterhouse-Five

Snow Falling on Cedars

The Sound and the Fury

Steppenwolf

The Stranger

A Streetcar Named
    Desire

The Sun Also Rises

A Tale of Two Cities

The Taming of
    the Shrew

The Tempest

Tess of the
    d'Urbervilles

Their Eyes Were
    Watching God

Things Fall Apart

To Kill a Mockingbird

To the Lighthouse

Treasure Island

Twelfth Night

Ulysses

Uncle Tom's Cabin

Walden

Wuthering Heights

A Yellow Raft in
    Blue Water